Financial Motivation
for Executives

Financial Motivation
for Executives

Graef S. Crystal

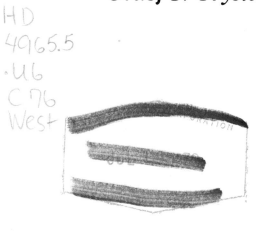

American Management Association, Inc.

International standard book number: 0-8144-5230-2
Library of Congress catalog card number: 77-116716

FIRST PRINTING

To Sheila

Preface

M ANY books have been written on the subject of executive motivation. Some are largely inspirational and others are extremely practical, dealing exclusively with money. Regrettably, the latter books on executive compensation imply that granting more money to an executive or adopting any gimmick which cuts his taxes is automatically motivational.

Meanwhile, a growing number of behavioral scientists have taken to the stump to declare that money of virtually any kind no longer motivates executives to perform.

Are the authors of mechanistic books on executive compensation right? Are the behavioral scientists right? Personally, I believe that neither are right.

Properly used, money can be highly motivational, but simply granting a little more money to an executive or finding a way to save him a few tax dollars is not necessarily proper use.

The purpose of this book is to examine the theories and principles of the behavioral scientists and marry them to the pragmatic aspects of executive compensation—in short, *to point the way to forms of executive compensation which are truly motivational and therefore beneficial to the company, its stockholders, and its executives.* The obituary for money, like that for God, may be premature.

If this book succeeds in demonstrating this premise, credit must go to a number of people who through the years have helped me to shape my thinking. Those whom I wish especially to thank are Algie Hendrix, James Budros, and Walter Carrell of General Dynamics Corporation and Joseph Kubert and John Lesher of Booz, Allen & Hamilton Inc. My thanks go also to Russell Moore, Planning and Acquisitions Editor of the American Management Association, who played midwife to this project; and to Dorothy Macdonald and Roberta Mantus, two of AMA's editors. If the product is smooth, it is only because they sanded away all the splinters.

Graef S. Crystal

Contents

1

A Philosophy of
Executive Compensation

AMERICA has become so successful economically that this book must perforce open on a defensive note. One price we have to pay for our affluence is the emergence of a host of individuals who claim that money no longer motivates. As critics of affluence, they have themselves become quite affluent. And so we have seemingly come full circle.

The Doctrine of Economic Man

Before discussing this "modern" development, let us go back in time. It was not too many years ago when all but a handful of the world's population lived at or below the subsistence level. These people were spared excruciating decisions as to whether this year's disposable income should be spent on a trip to Paris or on a new car. They had no disposable income. If they were able to avoid hunger on most days and provide shelter and clothing for themselves and their families, they counted themselves lucky.

As society made small advances, it became possible for a few citizens to give up "productive" work and devote themselves to studying the condition of their fellow men. Some of these individuals called themselves economists. They observed that when a man was not entirely certain that he would have enough to eat, he would tend to work as long and as hard as he could to obtain enough money to alleviate, if not remove, this uncertainty. Within the limits imposed by human physiology, this man would even double his hours of work to earn just a small amount of additional money. The fact that these additional hours were being recompensed at half time rather than time and a half or double time was immaterial because some additional money was always better than none no matter how hard one had to work to obtain it. Thus was born the doctrine of economic man.

Economic man, like the machines he was patterned after, was rational and seemingly devoid of emotions. It was always a certainty that he would take the steps necessary to maximize his income regardless of the effort it required. With economic man enshrined, the economists had an easy time of predicting future economic trends.

Time passed, productivity increased, and eventually most people in this country began to rise above the subsistence level. This evolutionary development was of little consequence for the doctrine of economic man, however, for these people had a large backlog of unsatisfied although not survival-related needs. Thus people were still interested in maximizing their incomes so they could buy a little more meat, own a second pair of shoes, and possess a roof that leaked only rarely.

The Affluent Society

More time passed. In the 1950s most people in this country had incomes which allowed them to live considerably above the subsistence level. They had meat every day, four and five pairs of shoes, and a roof that was watertight. In fact it became difficult for many people to decide how to spend their extra money.

The advertising industry rose to this new challenge. If people had no instinctual craving for an electric toothbrush or an automatic garage-door opener, they would have to be reeducated. Thus a new type of advertising industry was born whose purpose was to synthesize nonexistent needs. This led to John Kenneth Galbraith's "affluent society."

To the great distress of many economists, the doctrine of economic man showed some very distinct signs of morbidity in the new affluent society. No longer would most individuals accept a marginally lower rate of compensation just to earn a few extra dollars. Even with overtime pay at double time and triple time, it became more and more difficult to get a lot of "takers." (In periods of high inflation, as in the late 1960s, economic man shows signs of reviving, but this is probably temporary.) The stress in collective bargaining turned to more holidays, longer vacations, and other types of "time paid for but not worked." The ultimate horror to many conventional economists was to see blue collar workers negotiating for, of all things, *sabbaticals!*

13

Enter the Psychologists

Into this confused state of events rode the psychologists. Being free of any formal training in economics, finance, or general business, they were able to take a fresh point of view. They proceeded to study groups of white collar workers and professional employees to see what motivated them.

The psychologists developed a gimmick—that *money no longer motivates.* This was such a revolutionary statement that it really drew the crowds. Groups of executives, who on the surface appeared to be highly money-motivated, turned out to hear the "new wisdom." The speaking schedules of these psychologists became so busy that, in order to establish some semblance of priorities, many of them responded to requests for lectures by asking, "How much are you planning to pay?" Being academics, these psychologists saw themselves as exceptions to their own rule regarding motivation.

Even some of the more avant garde economists jumped on the bandwagon. John Kenneth Galbraith in *The New Industrial State* [1] remarked that he had yet to meet a corporate chief executive who would admit to working harder for more money. Apparently the executive was already working as hard as he could. (An unanswered question, however, is whether executives would work just as hard for more money—at a competitor firm that was willing to pay it.)

Perhaps the psychologists are right. But if they are, it is for the wrong reasons. If money no longer motivates, it is because of the inept way in which some companies

[1] Boston, Mass.: Houghton Mifflin Co., 1968.

14

handle their compensation programs. It is quite possible that the psychologists' studies were conducted at such companies.

In addition, the arguments of the "money is dead" school of psychology contain certain inconsistencies, which are discussed later. First, however, let us examine two other contemporary aspects relevant to the current value of compensation.

The Supply–Demand Crunch

We are today—and for the foreseeable future—in a seller's market for executive talent. As American business continues to grow, so does the number of executive positions. On the supply side of the equation, however, we find not an increase but a decrease owing to the low birthrate of the depression years. The "depression babies" are now 30 to 40 years old, and it is from this age group that most upper-middle management and lower-top management positions are filled. Thus we have the classic supply–demand crunch. The result has been inevitable: a rapid increase in the compensation levels of most executive positions.

Now academics are always criticizing American business for adopting purely pragmatic approaches to problem solving. Paying more money to obtain executive talent may be inelegant, and it may also be incorrect, but to the chagrin of those who claim that money no longer motivates, it works.

In another area, however, American business is heeding the advice of the academic community. For years, the management philosophers have been preaching that a good manager can manage anything. As Don Mitchell put it in *Top Man: Reflections of a Chief Executive*, "[The good

15

manager] can manage a bank, he can manage a railroad, and to the extent that anyone can, he can even manage the government." [2]

For years, too, the business community has rejected this advice on purely pragmatic grounds. If a steel manufacturer needed additional managers, why look for them in a bank? Obviously, one should get additional managers from other steel companies. This practice of industrial inbreeding naturally led to the payment of considerably varying compensation levels from industry to industry. As the supply–demand crunch hit certain industries, however, the going rate for new managers began to skyrocket and many executives became understandably concerned at the damage that these rates were doing to their precariously balanced internal equity. Faced with choosing the lesser of two evils, they therefore turned to managers in other industries—especially industries with lower compensation levels.

At about the same time, the conglomerate movement hit the United States and certain executives, who had previously been considered sound thinkers, began to assert their belief that the ability to manage assets was far more important than specific operating experience in a given industry. Thus the trend of hiring managers from other industries was given added momentum. (Banking, an industry characterized by low pay and a heavy stress on asset management, has become an especially attractive hunting ground for executive talent.)

Executive transplants, like organ transplants, went through a critical period. They had to face the autoimmunization reaction in their new company: a tendency to reject foreign tissue. These transplants were not given the benefit of modern immunosuppressive drugs, so only the most

[2] AMA, 1970.

hardy made it, came to be accepted by their host organization, and proved the theory that a good manager can manage anything. Thus an increasing number of executives are adopting, on pragmatic grounds, an approach which they previously had rejected on the very same pragmatic grounds. The result has been and will continue to be the attenuation of interindustry compensation differences.

Also at work today is a trend toward the attenuation of regional compensation differences. It is more common today for an executive to move from San Francisco to New York than it was 50 years ago for him to move from Newark to New York.

Still another trend has been the gradual elimination of any stigma resulting from job changes. The term "job hopper" seems to be leaving the language because it would have to be used on too many nice people nowadays.

Enter the Executive Recruiter

The fact is that changing jobs today is a painless process. It wasn't so long ago that a manager had to undergo a good deal of anguish and expend considerable energy in changing jobs. First, he had to prepare a résumé and hope his secretary wouldn't tell anyone. Then he had to peruse the classified sections of numerous periodicals, which contained mostly "blind ads." After sending out about 50 résumés and running the risk of sending one to his own company, he began an arduous round of interviews, which required his absence from work with a frequency that could attract attention. Finally, he *might* find a better job and switch companies.

People have a natural resistance to change, and obviously an individual had to be extremely dissatisfied with his current circumstances before he would overcome his instinctive inertia. Perhaps his original dissatisfaction did not even stem from his compensation level, especially since he had very little hard information on the compensation practices of other companies.

Today we have man's answer to the bee: the executive recruiter. Like the bee, he is busy and he pollinates. Now the executive has very little inertia to overcome in changing jobs. He doesn't even have to know he is unhappy! He merely sits by his telephone and lets the recruiter come to him. Thus the slogans "no fuss, no bother" and "one-stop shopping" have found a home in the employment field.

By providing competitors' compensation information ("they're willing to pay up to $50,000 base salary plus a healthy bonus and options"), the executive recruiter gives the executive the feedback he needs in order to evaluate the adequacy of his current compensation package. The executive who is euphoric concerning his compensation before the phone rings may be somewhat less euphoric after he learns that he can make 25 percent more at a competitor.

Thus the supply–demand crunch and the executive recruiter have combined to keep compensation alive and well as a motivator of human behavior in American business. Let us turn now to a discussion of basic principles which underlie a sound, motivational executive compensation program.

The Role of Taxes

Tax rates are probably not the most important element in compensation planning, but they are worth discussing first because so many people seem obsessed by them.

There is no question that the tax rates applicable to various compensation devices are of more than passing importance. Obviously, if two devices can satisfy a set of objectives and one can increase the individual's after-tax yield, that device should be adopted. But the big question is whether the alternative devices are in fact equally capable of satisfying a given set of objectives. Too many companies look first for any compensation device that promises a tax break; having found it, they clothe the plan with lofty purposes by way of rationalizing its use. Thus stock options are said to be highly motivational for a variety of reasons. As is demonstrated later, many of these reasons hold little water. The one compelling and irrefutable reason for adopting a stock option plan is to decrease the executive's tax rate. If it turns out that stock options are not motivating, well then, not everything has been lost!

For years, conservatives around the world have been decrying the high tax rates imposed on the wealthy, claiming that these rates would undermine executive motivation—and hence the economy itself. Yet, as long as the tax rates don't become truly confiscatory, executives seem to work just as hard. Is this an argument that money no longer motivates? On the surface, the answer could be yes, but as Galbraith points out in *The Affluent Society*, most executives place primary emphasis on their pretax compensation and not their after-tax yield. To them, their pretax compensation represents a form of recognition. (More is said of this later.)

The point here, therefore, is that companies should design compensation programs primarily to motivate executives to perform better. Then and only then should the companies turn to the question of taxes—an important albeit secondary issue.

This philosophy is particularly underscored by the passage of the Tax Reform Act of 1969, which embodies the most sweeping changes since income taxes were first enacted in 1913. A number of major executive compensation devices which previously had conferred important tax advantages on the individual executive have either been sunk by the new law or have taken on such a dangerous list as to make it prudent to abandon ship. Tax advantages and gimmicks are ephemeral, so this factor makes it all the more important to build a compensation package on the bedrock of real motivation rather than the shifting sands of taxation.

The Role of Cost-Effectiveness

Companies which have assiduously sought to lower the tax rates their executives pay have rarely considered whether such a process is efficient in terms of their own costs. Their implicit objective has been to put as many after-tax dollars as possible in their executives' pockets. But their objective should have been to put as many after-tax dollars as possible in their executives' pockets (leaving motivational considerations aside for the moment) *for the lowest net cost to themselves.*

People may disparage the efficiency of the federal government, but, when it comes to taxes, the government rarely gives something away for nothing. For example, a company can give a dollar of salary or bonus to an executive in a 50 percent marginal tax bracket for additional ordinary income, and the executive will keep 50 cents. This dollar costs the company only 52 cents because the dollar is deductible and 48 percent of its cost is passed on to the federal government (the current surtax rates are omitted from this discussion).

As an alternative, the company can give a dollar of capital-gains-taxed compensation to the same executive and he can keep 75 cents after payment of taxes at a 25 percent rate. This certainly seems better, which is why so many companies have adopted it. Yet these same companies fail to realize that they pay a price to grant capital gains income to their executives: They lose their own tax deduction because they cannot deduct income the executive pays capital gains taxes on. Thus it costs the company $1 to put 75 cents of after-tax income in the executive's pocket. The company could give the executive $1.50 of additional salary or bonus if it desires, and the executive, after paying ordinary income taxes at a 50 percent rate, still puts 75 cents in his pocket. With this approach, however, the company then has deducted the $1.50 of ordinary compensation on its own tax return and passed 48 percent of the cost onto the federal government. Hence, for the executive to receive 75 cents, the company's net cost decreases from $1 to 78 cents—or a 22 percent saving with no loss of after-tax income to the executive.

It is vitally important, therefore, that compensation alternatives be tested in terms of their cost-effectiveness with a view to minimizing the company's net cost per dollar of after-tax compensation to the executive.

Loyalty Versus Symbiosis

In the past, great stress has been placed on loyalty—loyalty to country, family, and company. Employees were told that their company loyalty would in time reap them great gains. It is particularly regrettable that loyalty has come to be so hollow a concept that many companies would do well to discard it altogether—or at least to play it down.

A more tenable approach to attracting, retaining, and motivating executive talent is *symbiosis*, originally a biological term the dictionary defines as a "union of two [animals or plants] which is not disadvantageous to either, or is advantageous to both." The term and the concept can be aptly applied to executive motivation. No longer is the talented executive in a totally subordinate and dependent position vis-à-vis his current employer, what with the supply-demand crunch and the emergence of the executive recruiter.

The bargaining power of the individual executive is approaching equality with his employer. Thus loyalty is out and symbiosis is in. Neither party can live without the other (and in some cases, neither can live *with* the other). Because of this, compensation plans should now be designed to encourage interdependence between the employer and the employee.

It is desirable in designing such compensation programs to assume that the individual executive is interested primarily in his own welfare and only secondarily, if at all, in the company's welfare. This is perhaps an overly harsh assumption, but once the company recognizes this fact it is less likely to get in trouble later on. The task, therefore, is to devise plans that would allow the individual executive to pursue his own self-interests both freely and unabashedly. And if in the process—accidentally, if you will—he assists the company in accomplishing its own objectives, then so much the better.

FOR EXECUTIVES

Risk Versus Reward

It is axiomatic in the investment world that reward must be commensurate with risk or no one will be interested in the particular security being offered. So, too, in the world of executive compensation must the reward equal the risk. That occupying a high executive position entails risk may not be a believable proposition to the academic community, but it is only too believable to the executive. This is especially true today, with the emphasis on performance and with the conglomerate giants lying in wait for the company that stumbles.

In Old Testament days, it was accepted practice each year for the high priest to transfer symbolically the sins of the people onto a goat and send him into the wilderness. Times really haven't changed all that much: Executives are our modern-day goats. If an executive is going to be penalized when things go wrong, whether he is at fault or not, then he must receive appropriate rewards when things go right. If executives don't receive recognition for their successes, the labor pool will largely be confirmed masochists.

Unfortunately, many companies are only too happy to affix blame but are seemingly loath to grant handsome rewards for excellent performance. Executives who receive little in the way of reward usually try to minimize their risks. Opportunities are thus lost and eventually the company stagnates—even founders.

At the executive level, a potential 10 percent merit increase is hardly a suitable reward for the risk being taken. Nor is a so-called incentive compensation plan that pays awards of 10 to 15 percent of base salary. If a company wants to attract gutty executives who are willing to take

23

chances, then that company must offer significant compensation when their decisions prove to be profitable. Saul Gellerman, in *Management by Motivation*,[3] correctly surmised that a large amount of money is needed today in order to "turn on" an executive with financial incentives.

The Role of Incentives

One of the best compensation systems is used in the sports and entertainment worlds. Pay is immediately and directly related to the contributions being made—at the time they are being made. Whenever Racquel Welch loses what it is that she has, she will no longer make $1 million per movie.

Universally adopting the sports and entertainment world compensation patterns, however, would create sheer chaos elsewhere in society. Most of us assume not only that our talents will fail to decline, but that they will indeed continue to increase indefinitely. As a result, we are unlikely to save during our great years to tide us over our poor years. Unhappily, there are far too many actors in "theatrical homes" because of their inability to plan ahead.

Society—and business also—demands that compensation have a modicum of stability. Thus we have the base salary. It is noteworthy that the word "base" can mean "the bottom of something, considered as its foundation" and "of little value." Judging from the way in which base salaries are handled by most companies, both definitions seem particularly apt.

[3] AMA, 1968.

It is well known that base salaries go up, but they rarely go down. And because they don't decrease, most prudent managers see to it that they don't increase too quickly either. Thus base salaries tend to be inert. To counteract the base-salary problems, years ago a number of companies devised what is known as the executive incentive compensation plan. (By attaching the word "incentive," the companies implicitly recognized that other plans, such as base salary and fringe benefits, contained little incentive.) By making these incentive payments go down as well as up, these companies were in a position to make total cash compensation (base salary plus the incentive) go down as well as up.

In adopting this approach, these companies were implicitly following accepted psychological stimulus-and-response principles first enunciated by Pavlov and then amplified by behaviorists.

Those who have raised children know that a spanking administered six months after an act of misconduct is likely to achieve nothing. Hitting the child with a 2 × 4 immediately after the misdeed will undoubtedly eliminate any recurrence of the act, but may eliminate the child as well. Similarly, a piece of candy given six months after a desirable act is likely to achieve nothing. A $100 bill given immediately after the act will probably be motivating but represents a case of overkill. The best way of handling a child is to give the proper amount of praise or punishment at the proper time, either to reinforce the things the child has done that are desirable or to eliminate the things that are undesirable. There has been no concrete evidence as yet that such an approach will not work equally well on executives.

Determining the Incentive Plan's Objectives

The key to such an approach is to determine what is desirable and what is not. In other words, just what is it that the company wishes to "incent"? In the business world, this question is answered all too easily by some executives: "Obviously we want profits." These executives unfortunately have failed to realize that although most incentive plans do motivate behavioral changes, the end result may be different from what they had anticipated. Two case histories illustrate:

> In an article in a reputable business magazine, a former plant general manager of an electronics firm is described as having given ". . . wide authority to decide which products [the plant managers] would make. Since each manager was evaluated on the basis of the profitability of his plant, the managers chose the products that were easiest to make—those already in production with high yields. Only reluctantly would the managers start new products."

> In a similar magazine, another article reported that a large conglomerate was having profit troubles in one of its major divisions. It was stated that "One reason, ironically, may have been an overemphasis on immediate profits. By tying managers' incentives to their current return on gross assets, the firm may have inadvertently discouraged them from spending enough on research and development."

Can the managers of these companies be blamed for their performance? Did the incentive plans at these companies fail? Surely the answer to both questions is a resounding no. The plans stressed current profits, and therefore the executives were motivated to maximize current profits. There was nothing in the plans about spending sufficient funds on research and development or on taking other steps to insure that the company was profitable *over the long term.*

In discussing these incentive plan pitfalls with certain executives, one may be chided for failing to take executive judgment into account. "My men aren't going to louse up the company's future by cutting their R&D expenditures just to get a few bucks more bonus. They're going to do what's *right.*" Yet sitting back and hoping that one's executives will do what's right is no way to run a company. Moreover, an incentive plan which requires executives to override the incentive aspects of the plan in order to do what's right can only be termed idiotic. A properly designed incentive plan should be a stepping-stone to accomplishment, not a hurdle placed in the executive's path.

The fact is that people see incentive plans through their own self-interested eyes, and therefore the company should be absolutely sure that it is encouraging its executives to do exactly what it wants done before initiating the plan.

In an effort to increase the number of its Christmas Club accounts, one bank recently devised a seemingly simple and appealing incentive plan. Each teller was to receive 1,000 trading stamps for each new account of $25 or more. Since most of the tellers were women, the idea of using trading stamps, rather than cash, was a masterstroke. The plan worked magnificently but somewhat differently from the way its designers anticipated. On the very first day, an officer overheard the following conversation between a customer and a teller.

Customer: I'd like to open a $500 Christmas Club account.

Teller (batting her eyelids): Sir, we're having a contest for Christmas Club accounts and I get 1,000 trading stamps for each account of $25 or more that I open. Would you mind terribly if I opened 20 new accounts for you?

Well, back to the drawing boards!

Personnel directors spend a good deal of their working lives making compensation surveys. At some point, they have probably learned that the personnel director makes considerably more in a company with a labor union than in one with no union. If they refine their data still further, they discover that a personnel director who deals with a militant union makes a good deal more than one who deals with a more pliable union. Ostensibly, the personnel director's job is harder when he has to deal with unions and therefore the pay is greater. Isn't a personnel director in a company with no union likely to wonder whether it would be more rewarding to see that his company's employees were unionized? And if the bargaining agent turned out to be the teamsters, so much the better!

Looking to the Long Term

Psychological research has shown that it takes less reward to motivate individuals toward accomplishing short-range goals than long-range goals. This is particularly true of Americans, for we are known around the world as a very impatient people. Most companies' incentive plans, unfortunately, are oriented toward the accomplishment of such short-range goals as current profits, as illustrated by the cases just mentioned. Yet increasingly complex technology forces us to take a longer and longer time to develop new products. These products require tremendous capital investments, often with no return for many years. Consider the case of The Boeing Co. In 1955, it decided to develop and produce a plane subsequently known as the 707. It was not until 1959, however, that the first plane was delivered to the airlines and not until 1965, some ten years after the original decision to produce the plane, that Boeing recorded its first dollar of profit on this fabulously successful aircraft. (It is worthy of note that when Boeing won the multi-billion-dollar supersonic transport (SST) contract, its stock dropped rather than rose. Investors correctly surmised that the project could only hurt Boeing's earnings over the short term.)

Most companies fall into the trap of basing their incentive plans on annual results simply because they must make annual reports to their shareholders. A plan based on annual results is valid only if the results and the decisions related to them were made in the same year. In many companies, continually longer product lead times have caused the decisions to be made in one year and the results to occur in another. A more viable approach therefore is to center an incentive plan around the company's typical product development cycle. Thus the plan might be oriented to achieving results two years, three years, or five years hence. That is not to say that rewards would not be paid during the intervening period, however, since the executives could receive either "progress payments" on future goals or payments for results stemming from past product development cycles.

Tying incentive systems to the accomplishment of longer-range corporate objectives has a significant side effect: The objectives themselves are likely to be established more accurately. The five-year plans of a number of companies are currently nothing more than exercises in extrapolation. For example, sales in 1969 were 20 percent higher than in 1968. Therefore, a 20 percent escalation factor has been used for each of the following five years. So it is with manufacturing costs, selling expenses, and profits. Such a plan looks good and gives the company an aura of progressiveness, but it accomplishes nothing. Indeed, it may obscure vital developments that, unless properly handled, will lead to trouble.

When management incentives are tied to future plans, however, there is less likelihood of a simple extrapolation because it could result in a significant loss of incentive compensation if it turns out to represent a spurious estimate of the company's future performance.

Keeping Rewards Meaningful

Once the objectives are properly established, the designer of a viable incentive system must provide significant rewards for the attainment of these objectives. As mentioned earlier, a payment of 10 to 15 percent of salary is unlikely to motivate most executives to take any significant business risks. Regrettably, few companies are willing to grant the significant rewards required. This results in the loss of valuable executive talent.

Take the case of H. Ross Perot, founder of Electronic Data Systems Corp. According to a November 1968 *Fortune* article, Mr. Perot first encountered the unwillingness of certain employers to pay for performance when he was still a boy. He had established a newspaper route ". . . in an area that the newspaper hadn't considered worth cultivating. Perot traveled 20 miles a day on horseback to deliver the papers, and because he had started the route, he received 70 percent of the price instead of the customary 30 percent. When the route began to thrive, the newspaper tried to reverse the ratio." The article goes on to indicate that Perot was successful in arguing the newspaper out of its plan. Later in his life, he was not so successful:

> The origins of this incredible bonanza [his founding of Electronic Data Systems] go back to the day in early 1962 when International Business Machines Corporation decided that Perot, one of its Dallas salesmen, was earning too much money. As Perot recalls it, IBM wanted to spread its commissions as evenly as possible among the salesmen, preferring not to let any individual make an inordinate amount. In 1962, Perot, who had joined the company in 1957, sold his year's quota of computers by mid-January. He then was kept in the office, where he found little to do but think subversive thoughts about his employer.

Mr. Perot subsequently put his subversive thoughts into action, much to IBM's detriment.

Some companies rationalize their failure to pay meaningful incentive awards by citing the specter of adverse stockholder reaction. One company president was visibly upset when 6 percent of his company's stockholders voted *against* a new incentive plan. Yet, not too long after, another company submitted a proposal to its stockholders to *reduce* the size of its incentive compensation funds and received the same 6 percent adverse stockholder vote!

Now, this is not to imply that one should overlook the interests of the stockholders and expect that they will approve any plan management cares to present. Stockholders are part of a symbiotic equation; they are looking out for their own self-interests, but at the same time they are dependent on company management. Therefore, they are likely to be attracted to only those plans that promise them a high percentage of the company's additional earnings. Except for the professional dissidents, few stockholders are likely to begrudge a company $5 million in bonus funds, if the funds are paid only when they receive $25 million in additional earnings.

Viewed in this light, incentive plans cost little or nothing when they lead to the attainment of the goals for which they were designed.

The Recognition Principle

Let us turn once again to those psychologists who say that money no longer motivates. They affirmed that motivation is a multifaceted thing. They discovered that some factors motivate primarily in a positive direction. An increase in these factors leads to greater motivation, but a decrease leads to little "demotivation." They also discovered that some other factors motivate in a negative direction. An increase in these factors does *not* lead to greater motivation but a decrease causes a good deal of *de*motivation. Working conditions, fringe benefits, and money belong in the second category. Such factors as the challenge of the job itself and recognition are considered motivators.

Few forms of recognition available to a company are as tangible as money. It follows that if recognition motivates and money can be used as a form of recognition, money can motivate.

Recognition is a relative phenomenon, however. Some individuals must receive a lot more than others for them to feel that they have received proper recognition. Cruel though it sounds, there can be no winner unless there are losers. It is questionable whether Olympic milers would run as hard as they do if everyone who crossed the finish line received the same gold medal and the same salute from the crowd.

A number of Communist countries are painfully aware that failure to use the recognition principle in compensation creates adverse results. Analyzing the low productivity of the Communist countries of Eastern Europe, *Time* magazine stated that "Under Socialism there is . . . almost no difference in pay between the worker who sweats over his machine and the non-worker who would rather flirt with shop girls, chat with colleagues, or take innumerable breaks. . . ." *Time* went on to report that a favorite expression among Communist workers is, "Whether you sit or stand, you make two grand."

It is regrettable that the compensation practices of too many companies in the United States bear an uncomfortable resemblance to those of Eastern Europe. At these companies everyone "gets a little something." And because everyone gets a little something, there are rarely enough funds left over to give the outstanding performers outstanding rewards. Of course, the outstanding executives may make 8 or 10 percent more than their mediocre counterparts, but they should be making 50 and 60 percent more if there is to be real recognition. The result is that the outstanding performers leave for greener pastures and the mediocre performers stay on. (Where else could they get such a good deal?) And it is the company that is ultimately the big loser.

Companies that are able to maintain significant compensation differentials between outstanding and mediocre performers seem to have less trouble in keeping executive talent over the short term—even when their overall compensation posture is below average—than companies whose compensation practices are above average but who consistently fail to provide the proper degree of performance recognition. This situation exists because individual employees, like the companies for which they work, are constantly surveying their "competitors" to assess the adequacy of their compensation. In this case, an employee's competitors are not in other companies, however, but are within his own firm. Hence, most employees make a point of finding out what their peers are being paid. Since they also have some well-defined opinions as to their peers' performance, they are in a position to determine, albeit subjectively, whether their own compensation is equitable. If an executive finds inequities, he becomes particularly susceptible to the blandishments of the executive recruiter when he calls to bring news of the compensation marketplace.

The Need for Guts

Most executives share two reactions in common when they are considering compensation increases (including bonuses) for their subordinates. First, most executives share the universal desire to be loved by everyone—or, to state the reverse, not to be hated. This pressure from below makes it exceedingly difficult for an executive to withhold an increase from his subordinate. Thus we have the so-called token increase, an award of generally 3 percent of salary or less. (There have been merit increases as low as $100 per year for a $25,000 executive.)

Second, virtually every executive assiduously cultivates an image of cost-consciousness. To be labeled a spendthrift is akin to damnation. This pressure from above makes it exceedingly difficult for the executive to give his subordinate much more than a 10 percent increase—and very often, his natural timorousness is reinforced by a formal company policy limiting compensation increases.

When confronted with pressure from above and below, many executives scuttle behind the average for safety. Thus, in many companies, if the average compensation increase is 7 percent of salary, better than 90 percent of all increases just happen to fall between 6 and 8 percent. The average, whatever other pitfalls it may possess, is always psychologically safe. Who, after all, can be criticized for granting an average increase?

Man's capacity to rationalize seems to be infinite, and virtually any rationalization that comes to mind will do when it comes to justifying a compensation action for an individual who should have none. Thus events outside the individual's control are used to explain why a small bonus is being given to someone who deserves no bonus at all. (How many times have you seen someone voluntarily relinquish a large bonus when events outside his control were the cause of his great success?) Or the fear is expressed that withholding a bonus, where one has been paid in previous years, will seriously compromise the individual's standard of living, notwithstanding the fact that he has been warned repeatedly not to count on the bonus.

Thus we have a leveling process in compensation. Where the range of merit increases should be between zero and 20 percent of salary, it is more likely between 3 and 10 percent. Where the range of bonuses should be between 15 and 75 percent of salary, it is more likely between 3 and 15 percent. The funds used to pay increases or bonuses to those who should have none necessarily come out of the pockets of those whose performance is outstanding, but unrecognized. After all, no company has an unlimited amount of compensation dollars to spend. Small wonder that the psychologists say money doesn't motivate!

As stated previously, the motivational value of compensation lies primarily in the recognition it bestows on the recipient. To achieve the spread of compensation actions that is necessary to afford the proper degree of recognition requires guts. It takes guts to withhold an increase or a bonus from someone who is undeserving. It takes guts to fight the system and get superlative rewards for a truly outstanding performer. Above all, it takes guts to recognize the handy rationalizations for what they are and to stay away from the psychological safety of the average.

Yet few of us seem to possess the kind of guts required. Take tipping, for example. In principle, we all endorse the belief that a bad waiter should get no tip and an excellent waiter should get a better-than-average tip—say 20 to 25 percent of the bill. But how many of us have the guts to "stare down" a hostile waiter confronted with an empty change plate? One way or another, most of us rationalize and pay him his 15 percent, promising ourselves that "the next time will be different." On the other hand, we are loath to pay the superlative waiter much more than 15 percent, because after all we have already spent plenty on the incompetents. Is it any wonder that excellent waiters are a rarity and that the restaurant industry suffers from a plethora of mediocrity?

Minimizing Turnover

The compensation objectives of virtually every company include the minimization of employee turnover. For all our sophistication in other areas, however, we still conceive of turnover as quantitative and not possessing qualitative aspects. The true turnover goal is not to reduce the absolute number of resignations but to reduce the number of resignations from outstanding personnel, while simultaneously increasing those from mediocre personnel. Compensation systems, if properly designed, can aid in attaining this important objective.

An effort should be made to see that one's outstanding personnel receive outstanding compensation compared not only with what lesser performers get within the organization, but especially with what one's competitors pay to their outstanding performers. Such an approach makes it highly difficult for a competitor to steal a superb performer, unless he is offering a significant promotional opportunity (and, from a compensation standpoint, there is no effective way to guard against this eventuality; like the Marines, a company should plan on taking at least some losses).

An effort should also be made to see that one's mediocre personnel are paid less than the minimum rates of one's competitors. (Of course, it is the rare company which has any mediocrity, having already weeded it out, but statistically there have to be as many mediocre personnel in the United States as outstanding ones, and they must be somewhere!) If these people subsequently quit, partly owing to their low salaries, the company gains from it because by again "drawing from the deck," it has a better-than-even chance of "improving its hand." And if these people quit to join a competitor, then the company gains a double advantage. Filling a Trojan horse with one's incompetent personnel and shipping it to a competitor is a promising and too-little-used business tactic.

Avoiding the Golden Handcuffs Approach

The stages of maturation of a typical company are very similar to the stages of human maturation. First, the new company has an entrepreneurial flavor, and its compensation program consists of very low base salaries and very high-risk compensation devices, such as stock options. As the company approaches adulthood, its compensation blend tends to approach the normal. The stability increases and the risks decrease. As the company becomes middle-aged, it tends, like middle-aged people, to concern itself with consolidating its gains and minimizing its risks.

It is at this point that many companies hit upon forcible income deferrals as the answer to their problems. These deferrals most commonly occur in the company's incentive compensation program, and the most common approach is to require that each bonus be paid not immediately but in a series of annual installments, starting either with the year of the award or after retirement. The rub is that any deferred amounts which have not yet been paid are forfeited if the individual voluntarily resigns. Thus these compensation devices have come to be known as the "golden handcuffs" approach.

Companies employing this approach euphemistically describe it as an incentive for the individual to remain with the company. From their standpoint this may well be true, but in the eyes of the individual it is a "disincentive" to leave and as such is almost uniformly resented. There is some evidence that the golden handcuffs approach actually does keep some people from leaving, but, by and large, the only thing that is consistently maintained is the level of employee mediocrity. Those whose performance is outstanding are easily "bought out" by a competitor. And since this motivational device is at best negatively oriented, an offer of employment involving a more positively cast motivational approach is all the more readily welcomed.

The fact that the individual's actual compensation is less than his nominal compensation during his all-important early years as an executive is still another reason why the golden handcuffs approach, far from keeping outstanding personnel, makes them increasingly receptive to the offers of the competition. To illustrate, assume that an executive with a $40,000 base salary receives a $20,000 bonus, payable in five equal annual installments. The executive's nominal total cash compensation is $60,000, but during the first year of such an arrangement, his actual cash flow compensation is $44,000, consisting of his $40,000 base salary and the first installment of his bonus. It is not until five years have passed and four more $20,000 bonuses have been granted that the executive is receiving the $60,000 the company says he is receiving. Meanwhile, the executive is highly susceptible to a competitor's offer of the same $60,000 total cash compensation if it is to be paid to him all at once.

Obviously, the problems with the golden handcuffs approach also work in reverse. A company that pays its bonuses in installments is undoubtedly going to have a tough time attracting an executive from a company that pays its bonuses in a lump sum.

Psychic Income

Not all elements in a company's compensation program can be measured in dollars. This is particularly the case with status symbols which provide a sort of psychic income to the individual and therefore must be considered within the overall framework of executive compensation.

Status symbols are used most frequently in such historical institutions as the army. This type of institution is generally characterized by high psychic income and low cash compensation. Although individuals obviously do not join the army solely because of its status symbols, there nevertheless appears to be some willingness to trade status for cash.

Status symbols lead a rather schizophrenic life in American business. On the one hand, evidence of their use is rife, what with posh executive offices which vary in size according to the level of the position, water pitchers, banana plants, limousines, and the like. On the other hand, there is a very vocal antistatus movement in almost every company. Some executives say that status symbols are completely useless; it's the size of the little old paycheck that really counts. They generally make such statements from behind a polished mahogany desk in their windowed, lushly carpeted offices.

Status symbols are alive and well in the executive suite. They fill a genuine human need, and so it is unfortunate that people who appreciate them are made uncomfortable by those who probably appreciate them even more but refuse to admit it. Status symbols are particularly important in business, because how else is one to tell the players apart? Wearing a tie used to have some distinction but it no longer does. And publicly revealing the size of one's compensation package is considered poor form in most social circles. (This is somewhat regrettable because if cash compensation is truly being used as recognition and is then shrouded in secrecy, its motivational value is diminished.)

A prime executive status symbol today is the qualified stock option. Although the amount of compensation it produces may bear little or no relation to the executive's performance, the fact that he has the option and is a "member of the club" bears significantly on his psychic income.

Far from being eliminated, therefore, status symbols should be exploited on a reasonable and well-controlled basis. Their continued use, despite constant criticism, shows their utility and durability. More important, they represent a relatively inexpensive form of compensation to the company. A $500 carpet placed in an executive's office (provided that not everyone has a carpet) may well be worth a good deal more than a $500 salary increase (although if he is asked, the executive will undoubtedly deny it), and in any event its cost, unlike the salary increase, is not borne every year.

The Need for Individualization

A growing body of research in the behavioral sciences has demonstrated that compensation is viewed somewhat subjectively and not always in direct proportion to the money involved. Two experiments, one providing direct evidence and the other indirect evidence, illustrate this finding.

1. A group of psychologists interviewed each employee of an industrial firm and asked him how much he thought the firm was contributing on his behalf to the company retirement plan. The employees, like those of most companies, had never been informed as to the amount the company was contributing, and thus they were forced to guess. The data analysis showed a distinct and not very surprising pattern: Younger employees consistently underestimated the company's contributions to the retirement plan, and older employees just as consistently overestimated them.

2. Children drawn from both high and low socioeconomic backgrounds were seated in front of a machine which could be manipulated to project a circle of light of any diameter on a screen. They were then asked to use their memory to adjust the circle of light until it approximated the size of a quarter. Almost uniformly, the children from low socioeconomic backgrounds made the quarter look like a half-dollar. Conversely, the children from high socioeconomic backgrounds made the quarter look like a dime.

Other experiments have shown that the value an individual places on various types of compensation changes over a period of time in accordance with his current needs. Thus the young executive who is raising three children hasn't the slightest interest in retirement income, but as he begins to approach retirement he is likely to change his opinion.

Because of these findings—and just plain common sense— some companies have begun to move away from an approach which dictates precisely how the individual's compensation package is to be structured and to offer him at least some degree of choice. Usually, this individualization first occurs in the company's bonus awards. The executive is permitted to choose from among various combinations of immediate cash and deferred income payments, and he can vary his choice from year to year. If he defers some income, he is often given the choice as to how such income is to be invested—say, in government bonds, company stock, or a mutual fund. He is also permitted to decide whether the dividends and interest received from the investments are to be paid to him in cash as they are produced or reinvested in the same types of securities from which they arose. Finally, the executive can decide when his deferred payments are to commence and the number of years over which the payout will occur.

Such an approach lets the younger executive with small children take his bonus entirely in cash to meet his pressing financial needs. As time passes and his income rises, the executive may decide to defer some portion of his bonus, with the payout slated to start when the children reach college age. At that time, the executive will probably revert to a total cash bonus; and by using this money plus the earlier deferrals, he can mitigate the financial burdens of sending several children through college at the same time. When his children finally become financially independent, the executive will probably elect to defer all of his bonus until his retirement. Of course, that is not always the pattern. On occasion, one finds the younger executive with substantial outside income and an accompanying desire to defer all of his bonus. One also finds the executive in his sixties who is still sending children through college and, although interested in providing more retirement income, simply can't afford it.

These exceptions wreak havoc with the "fixed choice" approach used by some companies as their answer to individualization. At these companies, all executives below, say, age 40 are paid their bonuses in cash. Those between 40 and 45 receive one-third of their bonus in cash and have the remaining two-thirds deferred. The ratio reverses between 45 and 50, and after age 50 the entire bonus is deferred. At other companies, a more elaborate matrix approach is used involving not only age but base salary and salary grade. These fixed-choice approaches offer a sort of planned individualization, but they still do not give the individual executive any real choice.

The Resistance to Individualization

If giving the executive a choice as to the form and timing of at least part of his compensation package makes such eminent sense, why has this approach not been universally adopted? One reason is usually given, but there is probably another reason also.

First, there is the argument that the administrative costs of individualization are prohibitive. With electronic data processing and a limited number of participating executives, this argument holds little water. One company which individualized its bonus plan reports that the whole process is handled by a single IBM card completed once each year and by a rather simple computer program. Of course, it will always cost something to individualize, but the benefits to be derived clearly outweigh these costs.

A less obvious but more real reason for opposing individualization is the authority that top management must of necessity relinquish to the individual executive. Some company presidents say, "Why should I give them a choice? All they will do is take everything in cash and squander it. Then they'll blame me for not providing for their retirement. No sir, I know what is best for my executives." It is somewhat ironic that these same executives who cannot be trusted to be reasonably prudent in managing their own financial affairs are assigned considerable responsibility for being prudent in the management of their company's affairs!

In today's environment of rising compensation costs and tight profit margins, executives who oppose individualization on essentially irrational grounds should reconsider their position. If one individual perceives $1 of retirement income to be worth $2 and another perceives the same $1 to be worth only 25 cents, it makes a good deal of sense to give the first individual a lot of retirement income and find some more appealing alternative for the second. In this way the company can lower its net costs of compensation and, as long as not every company is following the individualization principle, enhance its ability to attract and retain qualified executive talent.

One note of caution should be injected here, however. Some companies have adopted the individualization principle but have then tied it to the golden handcuffs approach. Thus the executive can take his bonus immediately in cash or can defer it, but if he chooses the latter, he stands to forfeit any unpaid installments in the event that he quits his job before they are received. Obviously, few executives are likely to accept this offer of deferrals. Such an approach therefore represents individualization in name only and generally causes nothing but resentment. It would be better not to individualize at all than to offer what amounts to a hollow promise.

Preparing for Obsolescence

Long ago, all companies discovered that machinery and equipment eventually wear out or become obsolete. And the greater the demands on the equipment and the faster the growth in technology, the more rapid the process. As a result, provision is made for accumulating reserves for the replacement of this machinery and equipment. Yet when it comes to executives, the same rules never seem to be applied.

There is equally abundant evidence that executives also wear out eventually. And the more the demands on the executive and the faster the growth in management technology, the sooner he becomes obsolete.

Most companies tend to take one of two approaches to meet this problem. The first approach is to reassign the executive to an innocuous position with a high-sounding title. Since this fools neither the executive nor his peers, a rather handsome salary increase is usually given also. That fools no one either.

Such an approach rarely works well. The executive generally knows that his performance is inadequate, for most of us, in our heart of hearts, have a pretty realistic picture of our abilities. The executive also knows that such an approach violates good management practice and should not be adopted. He knows further that none of his peers has been deceived by his new "promotion." These conflicts often make the executive feel insecure and angry. He does himself no good; he does the company no good and may actually hurt it by spreading his "poison" to others. Moreover, younger executives who believe that the company follows sound management practice are often disillusioned by such action.

FOR EXECUTIVES

The second approach is to beef up the company's retirement plan and liberalize the early retirement provisions. There are valid reasons for taking this approach, and they must not be discounted. Sometimes, however, the only reason a company has for improving its retirement plan is to eliminate executive deadwood by providing an incentive to retire early.

Restructuring a company's retirement plan to handle a few cases of executive obsolescence is like using an elephant gun to kill a fly. Retirement plan benefits cannot by law favor higher-salaried personnel, but must be applied uniformly to all—or almost all—the company's employees. The costs of using the retirement plan for this purpose are therefore staggering.

Both of these approaches have one characteristic in common: They are adopted by mediocre companies whose top management has no guts. Above all, it takes guts to face squarely a problem of executive obsolescence and remove the individual from the firm. Unfortunately, this is a cruel solution, especially when the executive has given the best years of his life in the service of his company and will probably suffer financially.

There is a more viable alternative that should be considered. Why not adopt a liberal executive severance policy which provides for salary continuation in the event of discharge (or what is known euphemistically as a management-initiated termination)? The length of salary continuation could depend on length of service with the company and could provide as much as full pay until normal retirement age for executives who are past the age of 55 and have been employed by the company for 20 years or more.

This rather simple approach will probably be met with two basic objections. First, it gives the executive something for nothing; it rewards incompetence. Yet giving the executive a fancy position with no real responsibilities or liberalizing the retirement plan to encourage early retirement can also be criticized for the very same reasons.

Liberalized severance payments will probably be criticized on grounds of cost also. Over a long term, these payments can build up to a considerable figure, and the costs could be incurred during the years when the company can least afford them. But why not establish reserves for executive obsolescence in much the same way that reserves are established for replacement of machinery and equipment? In effect, the company realistically estimates the amount of obsolescence it is likely to have and then sets aside a given amount of money each year to fund the severance plan. If such a long-term approach is taken, the costs in any one year should be minimal.

Although removing an obsolete executive may cost money, the costs will be even higher if the company retains the executive in a phony position and allows him to make a negative contribution rather than no contribution at all. The costs of liberalizing the retirement plan are of course still higher.

Basically, the company must face the certainty—not merely the probability—that executive obsolescence will occur. The company must therefore adopt an approach that will solve the problem at the least possible cost. Facing the problem of executive obsolescence is very uncomfortable, however, partly because the plan one develops may ultimately apply to oneself.

★   ★   ★

Twelve principles of sound compensation planning have been discussed in this chapter. Briefly stated, they are as follows.

1. Whenever possible, adopt plans that increase the individual's after-tax yield, but don't sacrifice motivation on the altar of taxation.

2. Consider not only the benefit to the executive where motivational considerations permit, but the cost to the company. Design plans that lower the company's net cost for a given dollar of after-tax compensation to the individual.

3. Establish a truly symbiotic relationship with executives rather than rely on their company loyalty.

4. Keep the reward commensurate with the risk.

5. Determine just what it is the company really wants and then "incent" it with meaningful rewards.

6. Understand the principle of recognition, and see to it that outstanding performers receive a great deal more than merely mediocre ones do.

7. Put less emphasis on minimizing total turnover and be more concerned with keeping outstanding performers and losing poor ones.

8. Avoid the golden handcuffs approach. Think positively, not negatively.

9. Stress the intelligent use of status symbols and other forms of low-cost psychological gratification.

10. Provide at least some degree of individualization in the executive compensation package.

11. Face and adequately prepare for the inevitable problem of executive obsolescence.

12. Above all, have the guts to follow all these principles.

2

Executive Position Evaluation

ESSENTIALLY, there are five variables which enter into the determination of an individual's compensation.

1. *Basic responsibilities:* the major duties which the executive has been assigned.
2. *Scope of responsibilities:* the size of the organization which the executive leads or to which he provides staff services.
3. *Supply–demand:* the differential value which the marketplace assigns to varying positions over varying periods of time.
4. *Industry:* the specific industry in which the executive is employed.
5. *Performance:* the manner in which the executive discharges the responsibilities he has been assigned.

Executive performance appraisal, which is discussed in Chapter 3, is concerned with variable 5. Executive position evaluation concerns the first four variables and is the subject of this chapter.

A number of approaches to determining the value of executive positions have been tried over the years, but today only two basic approaches are used by the great majority of companies. The first is the point-factor method and the second is the marketplace method.

The Point-Factor Method of Position Evaluation

The point-factor approach involves the initial determination of those factors which seem to explain why one position is more complex and more responsible than another. In practice, the number of factors seems to be limited only by the imagination of the designer. Thus we have plans with only three factors and some with as many as fifteen or more. Although each company assigns different names to the factors it has chosen, all the plans have separate factors for education and experience.

Each factor contains a series of descriptions which cover the various possible levels, or degrees, of that factor. For example, under education the degrees might be high school graduation, A.A., A.B. or B.S., M.A. or M.S., and Ph.D.

Each degree is assigned a number of points. For example, an A.B. degree might carry 150 points; an M.A., 200 points; and a Ph.D., 300 points. The maximum number of points available on any one factor (the points assigned to the highest degree) often varies from factor to factor, thereby causing some factors to have a higher weight in the overall point score. Thus, if the points assigned to the maximum

51

degree of each factor total 2,000 and those for the education and experience factors are 400 and 600, respectively, then education is implicitly assigned 20 percent of the total weight in the plan and experience, 30 percent.

The company's compensation personnel (sometimes a management committee) then analyze all the executive positions, using the point-factor plan. The applicable degree of each factor is chosen to match the characteristics of the position being analyzed and the points are totaled. Now we have a ranking of all the executive positions but are lacking their dollar value. That is the next step.

Certain executive positions are then chosen for survey purposes. As a group, they are called "benchmark" positions because the dollar values of the entire structure will eventually be tied to the value of these benchmark positions.

Positions are chosen as bench marks when the company believes that positions with a similar mix of duties and responsibilities can readily be found on approximately the same organization level in competitor firms. The distribution of bench marks is usually established so that there is a good vertical and horizontal cross-section of the company's organization: vertical through the various levels of management and horizontal through the various functional disciplines such as marketing, personnel, and engineering.

The salary rates paid by the firms surveyed are then plotted graphically against the already determined point values of the benchmark positions, and a trend line develops. This trend line permits a monetary value to be assigned to any given point value, even one which is not surveyed directly.

The last step in the point-factor evaluation process involves the grouping of point values into salary grades (for example, positions with 200 to 250 points are assigned to salary grade 4; positions with 251 to 300 points are assigned to salary grade 5) and the development of minimum and maximum amounts to be paid for each.

The point-factor evaluation plan, like all evaluation plans, has two major objectives: to insure that the company's salary structure is both internally equitable and externally competitive. Ostensibly, the point-factor plan achieves both these objectives, since executive positions are ranked internally, after which the ranks are anchored to the marketplace through a survey of competitive going rates. However, the value of point-factor plans is illusory.

In a properly designed plan, each factor should represent a discrete entity. What the entity measures should not be measured simultaneously by any other factors. Whether a point-factor plan actually consists of discrete factors can be determined by statistical factor analysis or intercorrelations. To illustrate, let us assume that 100 executive positions have been evaluated using a point-factor plan. The 100 different point values for factor A are then compared with the 100 different values for factor B. If the two factors are truly discrete, there should be no correlation (or at the very least a low correlation on the order of 0.2 to 0.3) between them. Similar correlations are also run between factor A and factor C, factor B and factor C, and every other possible combination of factors. Intercorrelations are also run between each factor and the total number of points produced.

The ideal point-factor plan produces a very low correlation between factors and between each factor and the total number of points produced. Regrettably, however, few point-factor plans even approach the ideal. Experience has shown that there is usually a considerable degree of factor

contamination in every plan, such that each factor cor-
relates rather highly (0.6 to 0.8) with every other factor
and with the total. Obviously, the factors used in these
plans are not measuring discrete variables but essentially
are measuring the same thing in different ways. In fact, in
most plans, all but one factor can be discarded (it makes
little difference which one is retained) and the points on it
can be used to establish the structure. The result would not
be significantly different from that produced by using the
multiple factors originally designed.

One company went to a lot of trouble designing an
executive point-factor evaluation plan. Being very conscientious, the compensation personnel decided to validate
the plan by comparing it with those of other companies.
So masses of information were compiled on each executive
position—including exhaustive position descriptions, organization charts, and work flow diagrams—and this information, which stood fully two feet high when as-
sembled, was sent to 47 companies. Each company was
asked to analyze the information on each position and
evaluate the position into a hypothetical salary structure
using its own method of position evaluation.

The results of this study showed that the company's
executive position evaluation plan was indeed a valid in-
strument in that its evaluations closely matched those of
the 47 companies surveyed. At least that was the conclusion
reached from a superficial analysis of the data. A more
detailed analysis, however, revealed that the 47 companies
used 47 different methods of evaluation. Some companies
had point-factor plans with three factors; some had plans
with ten factors; some had no factors at all. Yet, whatever
the method, all the companies came up with essentially the
same result. Again, a single, global evaluation factor, not a

54

series of discrete entities, seems to be operating in the evaluation process. The expert in charge of compensation at that company would have done well to discard his own plan (which was rather complex) and adopt the simplest plan being used by one of the groups surveyed. Since the results weren't going to differ very much anyway, he might as well have saved himself some work!

If point-factor plans were merely harmless and cost nothing but time, that wouldn't be too bad. But there is further evidence to suggest that most of these plans can cause serious damage to a company's conpensation program.

No matter what names are used, the great bulk of the weight in almost all point-factor plans is placed on education and experience. And, for a given level of education and experience, the points are going to be the same, regardless of what position is being evaluated. Thus, if the personnel vice-president's position calls for a master's degree and ten years of experience and so does the financial vice-president's position, both will receive the same points for education and experience. And both are likely to end up in the same salary grade because education and experience (factors which are the hardest to evaluate accurately) account for the greatest influence on the total point score. Unfortunately, such a conclusion is in direct opposition to what the marketplace says the positions are worth. Because of supply and demand, and perhaps other variables as well, a finance executive today earns a good deal more than a personnel executive.

If the company decides to peg the salary grade of the finance and personnel executives to the market value of the latter's position, it won't be long before the employee in the former position becomes a former employee! If, on the other hand, the company decides to peg the salary grade of the finance and personnel executives to the finance executive's position, it will have needlessly increased its compensation costs. Further needless costs will probably follow because the finance executive makes it a point to keep up with current compensation trends, and he knows he should be earning a good deal more than the personnel executive. It will never occur to him that he is amply paid and the personnel executive overpaid. All he knows is that he should earn more, and if the personnel executive is paid X, he naturally should be paid 1.5X.

A further problem with the point-factor approach to position evaluation is that it causes a mystique to be built up around the evaluation process. Of course, this is not a problem but an advantage for some individuals in the compensation field. When challenged by management in other disciplines as to why a certain position was evaluated in a certain salary grade, such individuals have been heard to reply, "You'll just have to take my word for it, because it would be impossible for a person with your background to understand the evaluation process without a great deal of study."

Such putdowns may be ego-gratifying to the individual doing the putting down, but they only hurt the compensation image of the company. Since managers in other disciplines have usually been excluded from any meaningful role in the evaluation process, they retaliate by fouling up the system. As long as their man has room to move within the assigned salary range, they appear to be content. But let him begin to close in on the maximum and the switchboard in the compensation department will light up. "I have assigned Sam some significant additional responsibilities in the last few months and I think that you should reevaluate his position. Obviously, it merits a grade 14 and not the grade

12 which it is currently assigned." If the manager gets his way, it won't be long before managers in other departments hear of this success story and begin to place their own form of pressure on the compensation group.

The point-factor approach also appears somewhat dishonest intellectually. The conscientious compensation analyst will confess that he is often astounded at the results produced by thoroughly objective evaluations made with the company's point-factor plan. "Why, that position can't be in grade 21," he says to himself, "it just has to be in grade 23." So he pulls down the shades, shuts the door, and "massages" his factor evaluations once again. After concluding that the position really requires a master's degree and not the bachelor's degree which he has assigned it, and that it calls for seven years of experience rather than the five he has assigned it, he manages—very scientifically, mind you—to evaluate the position into salary grade 23, *where it belongs*. Few individuals in the compensation field can deny having done the same thing—many times.

The Marketplace System of Position Evaluation

The marketplace appears to be a curious evaluator of executive positions—curious because the values the marketplace assigns to positions often differ wildly from those produced by most point-factor plans. But the marketplace is actually a wise evaluator.

During the depression, the highest paid discipline was marketing, which made a lot of sense then because business's main objective was to sell products to people who couldn't afford them and who were, to say the least, uninterested. During and shortly after World War II, the production

57

man came into vogue because in those days business's primary goal was to produce goods—whatever they were, and whatever the price, they could easily be sold.

Today, the financial man is in his prime, what with the trend toward asset management as evidenced by the conglomerate movement. Another field that is in its prime is electronic data processing. Programmers and systems analysts are courted as vigorously as this year's college all-stars —and this is reflected in the money they receive.

A company can, of course, pay anything it wants to for a given position, but not even the largest of companies, General Motors and American Telephone, are big enough to make the market in executive compensation. Ultimately, *a position is worth what the market says it is worth.* No amount of temporizing or rationalizing will alter this simple fact. Comments such as "computer personnel are overpaid" are based on someone's subjective impression of equity, are largely self-serving, and do no one any good. True, in the next world where equity is perfect, computer personnel will surely be paid less; but we are operating in this world, and the fact is that computer personnel are not overpaid but are paid what they are worth. Who says so? The marketplace says so!

The concept of letting the marketplace arbitrate the question of a position's worth is central to the second major method of position evaluation used widely by companies today.

The marketplace method of position evaluation consists of six basic steps. The first involves the selection of a number of benchmark positions. As noted earlier, these are selected for their commonality with positions at competitor firms and for their representativeness.

For survey purposes, the next step is to select a number

of competitor firms. A survey of the going rates paid the incumbents of these benchmark positions is the third step in the evaluation process.

The fourth step involves the design of a compensation structure to cover the positions that are to be evaluated. Taken alone, a compensation structure is nothing more than a series of numbers. It is obviously incomplete until the positions are actually assigned to various grades. Nevertheless, the distance from one point in a range to the same point in the next higher and lower ranges and the width of each range are significant and are built into the compensation structure design.

The fifth step is to place the benchmark positions in the compensation structure in accordance with their market worth.

The sixth and last step is to incorporate all the remaining positions into the structure based on a comparison of their duties and responsibilities with those of the benchmark positions whose market value is known and whose compensation grades have already been determined.

Let us now turn to a more detailed examination of each of the six steps.

Determining the Number of Bench Marks

How many benchmark positions should the company select for survey purposes? The answer to this question is governed by pragmatic rather than theoretical considerations, since the number of potential bench marks (that is, those positions whose mix of duties and responsibilities is common to many companies) is typically much larger than the number that can actually be used. The fact is that compensation personnel in the companies to be surveyed simply will refuse to tolerate a survey with an inordinately large number of benchmark positions. The resistance to participation in a survey generally rises with the square of the number of positions included in the survey, and the point of no return is reached around the 30-position level. Beyond that point, a company is likely either to refuse to participate or to give the survey short shrift, such that the gains in quantity of responses will be offset by a loss in quality.

Preparing the Survey Questionnaire

Having selected the benchmark positions, next we must prepare the survey questionnaire. The detail that this questionnaire should contain is partially dependent on whether the survey is to be conducted by mail or by personal visits to the participating companies. Time and money permitting, there is no question that personal visits are far better for producing high-quality data—and especially for controlling for comparability (the correct matching of positions on the basis of duties and responsibilities).

The survey questionnaire is essentially divided into two parts. The first part seeks general information on the company and the types of compensation plans it has. Since most of this information can be derived from published data, this part of the questionnaire serves as a checklist for materials to be obtained, such as annual reports, proxy statements, organization charts, copies of incentive compensation plan and stock option plan texts, and copies of group insurance, profit-sharing, savings, and retirement plans.

The second part of the questionnaire is devoted to a

survey of the benchmark positions. A position description must be prepared for each position; its length depends on whether the survey is to be conducted by mail or by personal visits. If the latter approach is being utilized, a "capsule" position description will suffice—one of three or four sentences which sets forth only the major responsibilities of the position and in effect captures its essence. If more details are required to facilitate position matching, these can be readily provided during the personal interview.

A data sheet for each position is included in the questionnaire to elicit compensation and position scope information. Typical compensation data being sought include:

* Number of incumbents.
* Formal range of base salaries, if any.
* Range of actual base salaries, if there are two or more incumbents.
* Actual average salary.
* Incentive compensation awards for the past two to three years, including date and amount of award (and range of awards if there are two or more position incumbents).
* Stock option data for each incumbent, including date of grant and option price per share.

Some conventional data techniques should be mentioned at this point. Base salaries are usually expressed in annual terms for executive personnel and at the rate in effect as of the date of the survey (rather than the "W-2" rate for the preceding year).

Incentive compensation awards, on the other hand, are expressed as the total amount accrued for the year in which the award was earned, rather than the year in which it was paid. Thus a bonus of $10,000 paid in February 1969 but attributable to 1968 performance is listed as a 1968 bonus. If the bonus is paid in five installments and the first installment is only $2,000 (or perhaps the entire bonus is being deferred until retirement), the amount to be reported is still $10,000; that is, the amount that was *earned* even if not yet paid. Thus the total cash compensation (base salary plus bonus) reported for a given incumbent often differs from his true cash flow compensation.

To obtain a realistic picture of stock option grants, data must be sought for at least the five-year period preceding the date of the survey. This is because stock options, unlike salaries and bonuses, are not necessarily granted every year. Although the payment pattern may be annual in some companies, at others the grants are made sporadically. Nevertheless, most companies with option plans make a grant to a given executive at least once in any five-year period, since five years represents the maximum span of exercise permitted under qualified stock option plans. (If the company utilizes a nonqualified plan with a different maximum span of exercise, option data should be sought for the particular period of exercise rather than for the five-year period.)

Position Scope

Position scope information is vitally important in any executive compensation survey. As a company expands, it typically increases the number of lower-level personnel. On the other hand, the number of executive personnel is likely to remain unchanged. But each executive's responsibilities are expanded. Thus, if the company doubles in size, there is still likely to be only one financial vice-president. He will have a tougher job, however.

A number of years ago, correlation studies were performed on the relationship of executive compensation to a number of position scope variables, such as organization sales, profits, invested capital, and assets. Sales proved to be the variable that was most highly correlated with executive compensation payments, and thus it has come to be the accepted measure of position scope. This is somewhat regrettable since there is considerable evidence to indicate that a multiple correlation or multiple regression analysis relating many variables (such as sales plus profits plus market value of stock or all of these expressed as a percentage of assets) to executive compensation payments would improve the correlation considerably and account for much of the variance around the mean. Indeed, Stanford Research Institute tried such an approach with engineering compensation, and its early research showed great promise. Many companies, however, view multiple correlation as an overly sophisticated technique, and hence it has met with considerable resistance.

One result of any survey technique is feedback on executive decisions. Thus, when the original single variable correlation studies were first performed, the correlation of profits to compensation (about 0.75) was very close to that of sales to compensation (about 0.80). As noted, sales became the chosen position scope variable, and all other variables, including profits, were dropped by the wayside. Since there is abundant evidence that companies base their compensation actions at least partly on survey data, there has been a trend over the years toward increasing the correlation between sales and compensation. In effect, one president looks at a sales–compensation curve and notes that his man is below the curve line. He therefore reasons that increased compensation is in order. Similarly, another president notes that his man is above the curve line. He therefore reasons that he should slow down on increases for this individual until the curve catches up with his compensation.

Both presidents are, of course, seeking the psychological safety of the average, and, depending on the performance contributions of their subordinates, both may have made a grievous error in using average compensation as their target. Nevertheless, the result has been a narrowing of the dispersion around the mean and hence an improvement in the correlation between sales and compensation. By the same token, there has been a decrease in the correlation between compensation and other variables, such as profits. This kind of feedback result, if true, is unsatisfactory in terms of motivating executives to seek increased profits rather than increased sales. (On the other hand, such a result is in line with John Kenneth Galbraith's thesis, developed in *The New Industrial State*, that companies today are oriented more toward growth than profits.)

Although sales is the standard measure of position scope, there is no reason why the surveying company should not obtain other measures, if for no other reason than to serve as a cross-check on the sales measure. These other measures can and will vary according to the position being surveyed. Thus, for a financial position, information could be obtained on assets controlled. Volume of production might be the measure sought for a production position. Location in the organization hierarchy is of course a type of scope measure also and should be obtained on every position.

All position scope measures should be based on the scope of the position being surveyed and not necessarily on the scope of the company itself. For example, if a division manager in a $1 billion company is responsible for $200 million in sales, then $200 million and not $1 billion is the correct measure of his position scope. Only corporate staff positions (excluding group executives who are measured on the group's sales) are measured by total company statistics.

At this point, one may ask, "Why take the time and go to the expense of conducting a survey? Why not make use of available published data?" The answer is that the company should perform a custom-tailored survey as well as use available published data.

The marketplace method of position evaluation rests on a foundation of valid data on competitors' going rates. Published survey information unfortunately cannot provide a strong enough foundation, since position comparability is generally looser; the surveys are conducted by mail, thus allowing interpretive errors to creep in; and the mix of participating companies cannot be controlled. As a result, the company may receive some information on its competitors by using a published survey, but it may also receive information that it doesn't want and that distorts the overall survey figures.

On the other hand, the value of published survey information should not be discounted entirely, because it is based on a much larger sampling of companies than any single company could easily obtain and hence contains a good degree of year-to-year reliability. This information therefore should be used when compiling marketplace statistics for evaluation purposes; its role will be discussed shortly. Two excellent sources of broad industry compensation statistics are the American Management Association's Executive Compensation Service and a survey known as Project 777. The former can be purchased by companies that have not actually taken part in the survey, although participation is encouraged. The latter, a survey of companies with divisionalized organization structures, requires participation as one of the prices of admission.

While the company is preparing its survey questionnaire, it should also be deciding on the companies it wishes to have participate. Generally, there should be no fewer than ten such companies, since with a smaller number one company may have too great an influence on the overall survey results. From a practical standpoint, the maximum number should be about 15.

Picking the Survey Participants

The companies selected for participation should represent a good cross-section of the surveying company's competition. This means that both "product" competitors (those with which the company competes for sales) and "people" competitors (those with which the company competes for people) should be included. Particularly important are "double threat" competitors that compete for both products and people.

Selecting a company for a survey and getting it to participate are two different things. Resistance, however, is never as high as most people think, because compensation practices are relative, not absolute, so all companies have to depend on other companies to validate their own compensation practices. Nevertheless, a company is likely to find few takers unless it offers a summary of the findings to the participating companies so that they can get something in return for what they have given. This summary usually keeps company identities confidential (Company A, Company B, and so on) so that none of the participating companies can identify which response belongs to which company.

In this regard, considerable care must be taken to insure that the summary is indeed confidential, for there are many ways to break the code. For example, corporate sales, when used as a position scope variable, are a dead giveaway to anyone with a copy of the *Fortune* 500 list. Similarly, dates of option grants and option prices can be traced through published stock market data.

One further point should be mentioned with regard to selecting the survey participants. It is best that all have the same bonus practices as the surveying company now has or is about to adopt. That is, if the surveying company has a bonus plan (or is developing one), the participants should also have bonus plans. If the surveying company does not and will not have a bonus plan, then none of the participants should have a plan. (Of course, some absolutely key competitors with practices different from those of the surveying company may simply have to be included.) The reason is that base salary practices of bonus-paying companies differ considerably from those of non-bonus-paying companies. More is said of this shortly.

It is also worth emphasizing that in any survey, position comparability is the dependent variable and compensation is the independent variable. That the reverse sometimes occurs can be illustrated by one experience of a compensation specialist. The compensation director of another company invited him to participate in a survey a number of years ago, and he accepted. The director indicated that this survey would feature very closely controlled position comparability and that as a result he would send the specialist detailed position descriptions in advance and then follow up with a personal interview. The specialist read the position descriptions, and when the director arrived they began to exchange data. The director started with the first position and proceeded to amplify on the written position description to be sure the specialist understood exactly what the position was all about. The specialist replied that his company had an identical position and explained all its duties and responsibilities. The director said, "That's perfect. Now, we pay our position $20,000 per year. What do you pay?" "We pay $15,000 per year," the specialist answered. There was a long pause. "Well," he said, "don't you have a higher-level position that pays around $20,000 per year?" In effect, he was looking for confirmation of his company's current practices; and if this required that position comparability be bent a little, so be it!

Establishing Market Worth

After the survey is completed, the next step is to analyze the data and determine the correct going rates of base salary and total cash compensation to be used for evaluation purposes. Before doing so, however, the company should consider whether there is a need for more pieces of survey data to reflect the movement in market rates between the time the information was first reported and the current date. Such a course of action will probably be required only if a relatively long time span (six months or more) intervened between the time the first company was visited and the time the survey was completed. It is more likely that it will be required only with the supplementary published survey data, because such data usually contain a considerable time lag.

The percentage to be applied for this purpose should be conservative. If, for example, it is believed that compensation rates have been increasing lately at the rate of 5 percent per year, then a 4 percent annual rate of escalation should be adopted. Two basic analytical techniques, one descriptive and the other graphic, can be used.

Descriptive analyses. Descriptive techniques consist of the calculation of medians or averages and are useful when position scope is not a relevant factor; that is, when virtually all the positions have essentially the same position scope. Three basic averaging techniques may be employed.

The first is a simple unweighted average where each company's compensation information for a given position is added together, and the resulting figure is divided by the number of companies in the survey. Although it seems obvious, the surveying company should never include its own information in compiling going rates. For some reason, this mistake is frequently made. The surveying company's own information should, however, be used in preparing the summary for the participating companies.

The second type of average, which is weighted by population, is useful when there are multiple incumbents for each company's position. Each company's average compensation for that position is multiplied by the number of people holding that position, and then the resulting figures are added together and the total is divided by the total population of all the companies.

A third technique, which is rarely used but can be extremely valuable, is to calculate a "judgmental average." From a conceptual standpoint, it is closely related to the weighting techniques described later for performance appraisal. Essentially, the first average described—the unweighted average—does carry some implicit weights. In effect, if there are ten companies in the survey and an unweighted average is employed, each company is implicitly being assigned 10 percent of the total weight. This may or may not be an accurate representation. Perhaps one or two companies pose a particularly competitive threat to the surveying company; and one or two others, while still important, are less of a threat. If such is the case, a judgmental average can be useful.

The analyst first determines the average weight per company by dividing the number of companies into 100 percent. He then increases this average weight for the more important companies and decreases it for the less important companies such that the total always remains 100 percent. He then multiplies each company's compensation data by its assigned weight, adds the resulting figures, and divides by 100.

When used in connection with an unweighted average, the judgmental average provides a good indication of the influence that the most and least important companies are having on the overall going rates. This approach is also especially valuable in that the weighting patterns can be changed from position to position to reflect the fact that a given competitor does not pose the same threat in every situation. For example, a people competitor may be given a very high weighting on EDP executives because the market for these individuals transcends industry lines, and a company that can offer employment without physical transfer is bound to be a bigger threat than one that requires a 2,000-mile relocation. On another position, however, the same competitor may receive a very low weighting because incumbents are rarely observed to cross industry lines.

Graphic analysis. If the position being analyzed does

FOR EXECUTIVES

contain responses involving widely differing position scopes, a graphic approach should be employed. To illustrate, let us assume that organization sales are going to be used as the measure of position scope. For that position, each piece of compensation information is plotted graphically against the applicable sales figure. Log-log graph paper is preferred, since the relationship between sales and compensation is essentially logarithmic rather than linear or semilogarithmic. Compensation data should be plotted on the vertical axis (Y axis or ordinate); and sales data should be plotted on the horizontal axis (X axis or abscissa).

Once the scatter diagram is completed, a curve (actually a straight line on log-log paper) must be plotted to derive the trend of going rates. Preferably, this curve will be derived through a statistical least-squares analysis, although it can sometimes be plotted visually without untoward consequences, inasmuch as the sales–compensation curve is often not that terribly sensitive. Exhibit 1 illustrates the graphic approach.

The going rate for the surveying company's position is read from the curve by referring to the organizational sales for which the surveying company's position is responsible. If desired, this going rate can be judgmentally averaged with similar curve information from published surveys. Obviously, the greatest weight should be placed on the custom-tailored curve.

It is worth repeating that compensation surveys, like other statistical techniques used in the compensation field, are subject to at least some degree of standard error. Therefore, the true average is just as likely to lie within plus or minus 3 to 4 percent of the computed average as at the computed average point itself. Simply because the surveying company's compensation payments are 3 percent below the survey averages does not mean, then, that the company is truly below average and must take some remedial action.

Designing the Compensation Structure

At this point, the survey has been completed, the data have been analyzed, and going rates of salary and total cash compensation have been computed. The next step is to design a compensation structure.

Exhibit 1 **Typical organization sales/executive compensation curve.**

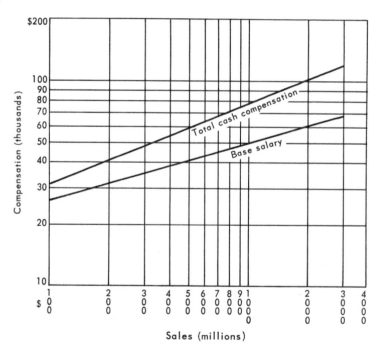

The practice at most companies is to design only a salary structure and then pay bonuses as a percentage of current base salaries. The danger in such a practice is that it may lead to a pyramiding of compensation such that the individual with an outstanding base salary receives an outstanding bonus percentage applied to his salary. Thus he has unwittingly been paid more than once for the same performance contributions.

For that reason, a total integrated compensation structure is preferred, with each range containing five points: (1) base salary minimum; (2) base salary control point; (3) base salary maximum; (4) total compensation control point; and (5) total compensation maximum. Of these five points, the two on which the entire structure is anchored are the base salary control point and the total compensation control point.

It was indicated earlier that companies with bonus plans or those about to adopt one should confine their surveys to other companies with bonus plans. The reason is that bonus-paying companies consistently pay lower base salaries than non-bonus-paying companies. When bonuses are added, however, the total compensation is consistently high. Thus we have a good example of the principle of risk versus reward.

If a company with a bonus plan surveyed some companies with no bonus plans, this would raise the average going rates for all companies combined. If the company then designed its salary structure around these higher going rates and added a bonus equal to the average of bonus-paying companies, the result would be needlessly high total compensation.

Base salary control points. The buildup of the compensation structure starts with what will eventually become the base salary control point. A number is picked to represent what will probably be the lowest going rate for any executive included in the structure. Then a series of additional numbers is generated, each higher than the preceding, until a number is reached that will be the highest going rate for any executive included in the structure. These numbers are generated exponentially, with each number a certain percentage higher than the preceding number.

The proper percentage spread between control points is a matter of considerable controversy in the compensation field. One school of thought maintains that the spread should be low (say, a uniform 5 percent escalation) so that the decision to evaluate a position one grade higher or lower than is initially recommended will cost the company very little. There are two problems connected with this approach. The number of compensation grades produced is usually very high, with the result that the structure may become administratively unwieldy. Moreover, if it is too easy to "give up" a grade, such an action will probably occur with discomforting frequency.

Therefore, it is preferable to employ a constantly escalating structure approach. Generally, the lowest control points will be about 6 to 7 percent apart, with the percentage increasing gradually to around 10 percent at the $30,000 to $35,000 salary control point level.

Total compensation control points. Now we have a stream of numbers which eventually will become base salary control points. The next step is to generate a stream of numbers which will eventually become total compensation control points. One approach is to assign positions to the structure solely on their base salary going rates and then establish an average bonus percentage for each position such that the summation of (1) the base salary control point plus

(2) the base salary control point times the average bonus percentage would equal the average total compensation derived for that position from the survey data analysis. The problem is that the average bonus percentages for various positions contain mild and insignificant variations which have nothing to do with the position level but which result from the relatively small sample sizes. Thus two executive positions have the same base salary control point, but the survey data show that one should earn an average bonus of 50 percent of base salary and the other an average bonus of 45 percent of base salary. Although the survey data show that these differences do exist, one would have a time of it trying to justify such an approach to the two executives involved!

Therefore, average bonus percentages must be smoothed —or normalized—before the total compensation control points can be generated. To do this, each bonus in the entire survey (regardless of position) is plotted as a percentage of salary against the corresponding base salary. Using log-log paper, a curve is derived from the scatter diagram. Such a curve from a survey of some 50 companies is shown in Exhibit 2. (The reason why the bonus as a percentage of salary increases with increasing salary is explained later.)

For each base salary control point, the appropriate bonus percentage is determined using the normalized bonus curve. This percentage is then applied to the base salary control point, the resulting figure added to the base salary control point, and we have the total compensation control point. Thus, if a given base salary control point is $30,000 per year and the normalized bonus curve shows a 27 percent bonus, the resulting total compensation control point for that base salary control point is $38,100 ($30,000 + [$30,000 × 27%]).

At this stage, the company has a series of base salary control points and total compensation control points which insure that it will properly track the competition. That is to say, an average performer will receive an average base salary, and he will also receive an average bonus. His combined salary and bonus will also equal the competitive average total cash compensation.

Restricting Bonuses to Above Average Performance

Do companies want to reward average performance at all? Some companies, for example, will object to paying any bonus to an executive whose performance is only

Exhibit 2 **Relationship of executive bonuses to base salary.**

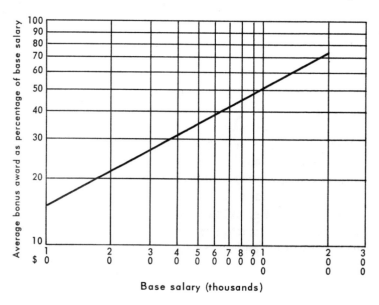

average. "We want to pay bonuses only for outstanding performance," they will say. These companies have therefore adopted the implicit stance of making their base salary control points the equal of the average total compensation control points. In that way, the average performer receives a salary which equals the average total cash compensation paid by other companies. Theoretically, there is no necessity to pay this man a bonus unless and until his performance rises above the average. Although such an approach is seemingly appealing, it has two pitfalls.

First, it violates the principle of the greater the risk, the greater the reward. To illustrate, let us assume that our survey shows a given position carrying an average base salary of $40,000, average total cash compensation of $50,-000 (thus a 25 percent bonus), and maximum total compensation of $60,000 (that is, the highest-paid individual in this position typically receives $60,000 per year). The concept of paying salaries equal to average total cash compensation presents no problem when the executive's performance is average, but there is a significant problem when his performance is below average, above average, or outstanding. If, for example, our hypothetical executive received an outstanding performance rating, he would, under the system used by some companies, receive a $50,000 base salary (equal to average total cash compensation) and a $10,000 bonus. His total compensation would therefore equal the maximum total compensation presumably paid to outstanding performers at other companies. The figures are right, but our hypothetical executive got a pretty good deal! He received the same total reward as his outstanding counterparts at other companies but he took less risk because his salary, representing assured income, was $10,000 higher per year. Similarly, if the executive's performance is below

77

average, and he therefore receives no bonus, he still earns $10,000 more than his less efficient counterpart at competing firms. For that reason, establishing base salary control points to equal average total cash compensation should be avoided.

Another factor to consider in this regard is that, for reasons discussed later, most companies do not confine their bonuses to cases of outstanding performance but give virtually every executive a bonus each year. This applies not only to companies that pay bonuses for average performance but also to companies that say they pay bonuses only for outstanding performance. Thus the company that establishes its base salary control points to equal average total cash compensation is likely to pay awards even to its average performers. The result is a pyramiding of compensation that costs the company money but gives it little or nothing in return.

Paying Above Average Compensation as a Matter of Policy

Another group of companies will reject the base salary control points and total cash compensation control points generated in the manner just described because, as they put it, "Our policy is to pay above average compensation. Therefore, the control points should be increased by 10 percent [or some such figure]." Such an argument is utterly without merit. No company should ever pay more than others for average performance. The only possible benefit to be derived is an increased ability to hold average performers, and, statistically speaking, these are not hard to find in the event that turnover does increase. All the company does is greatly, and needlessly, increase its compensation costs.

The only time a company's aggregate compensation costs should be above the average of its competitors is when its mix of excellence is also above the average of its competitors. And this should be verified by referring to hard financial performance figures.

Creating More Reward Through Increased Risk

There is an alternative approach which does have merit and can be adopted by the gutty company. It is to decrease the base salary control points and increase the total compensation control points. The risk-reward principle dictates, however, that the exchange ratio be somewhat higher than one dollar of increased bonus opportunity for one dollar of decreased salary opportunity. As a rule of thumb, this approach should employ a two-for-one principle. To illustrate, let us assume once again that the competitors' average base salary is $40,000 per year for a given position and that their average total cash compensation is $50,000 per year. Let us further assume that those are the control points developed in the manner just described. A company could, if it desired, decrease the base salary control point by 10 percent—or $4,000 per year in this instance. Using the two-for-one principle, the total compensation control point would be increased by $8,000, such that the new base salary control point and the new total cash compensation control point would be $36,000 and $58,000 per year, respectively.

This approach can help the company reduce its fixed costs and keep its total compensation payments more in line with its ability to pay. It also offers the individual executive an opportunity to receive total compensation which is substantially in excess of industry levels at performance levels of average or above. But the individual executive also takes a risk, in that if his performance is poorer than average, he will receive total compensation (in this case a salary alone) which is less than that provided by the competition.

However, the larger the award opportunities, the stronger must be the company's performance appraisal infrastructure. (This is discussed in the following chapter.) And the company must be more willing to employ this infrastructure in making gutty performance assessments. Without these factors, the use of below average base salary control points and above average total compensation control points is a waste of time.

Mention should be made here of the principle of salary "discounting." People have said that base salary control points established to equal something less than average total compensation represent a discounted salary structure. This is not an automatic case of discounting, since the base salary control points may still equal the average base salaries paid by other companies with bonus plans. It is preferable to restrict the term "discount" to the approach described previously where base salary control points are actually reduced below the level of average base salaries paid by other companies with bonus plans.

Establishing Minimum and Maximum Range Points

Let us assume that the company has decided to adopt conventional base salary and total compensation control points. The next task is to determine the base salary minimum and maximum points and the total compensation maximum point.

These figures can be derived from the salary and total compensation dispersion observed in the survey. If this survey is typical, it will show that the dispersion around the mean is somewhat asymmetrical. Thus the dispersion below the average runs out of gas (or goes spurious) at about 80 percent of the average figure. Above the average, however, this does not occur until about 130 percent of the average figure. This 130 percent guideline applies to both salary and total compensation frequency distributions.

One approach, then, is to derive the remaining three range points in the following manner:

1. Base salary minimum—80 percent of the base salary control point.
2. Base salary maximum—130 percent of the base salary control point.
3. Total compensation maximum—130 percent of the total compensation control point.

The first and third of these figures present no problem but the second does: Where should the above average to outstanding performer look for his rewards? To his base salary *and* his bonus? Or to his bonus alone?

A logical answer is that the great bulk of rewards for above average to outstanding performance should be placed in the bonus, because such an approach offers potentially more motivation. Therefore, the base salary maximum points should be reduced below what the survey would justify (say, 120 percent of the base salary control points), and, using the two-for-one principle, the amount of the decrease should be doubled and added to the total compensation maximum points.

This approach presents the danger of drastically overcompensating the outstanding performer. This is not cause for much concern, however, because, as noted earlier, one of the objectives of any sound compensation program should be to reduce turnover among the company's outstanding executives (rather than simply reduce total turnover).

In the field of psychology there is a concept known as cognitive dissonance, and some psychologists advocate that it be applied to compensation. The theory is that if an individual is deliberately overpaid, he will perceive a dissonance between his position and performance on the one hand and his compensation on the other. Since this may cause him to feel guilty, he will redouble his efforts to bring his performance into line with his compensation, thereby removing the source of dissonance. Perhaps an outstanding performer who is paid substantially more than outstanding performers in other companies will, because of his perceived dissonance, make an even greater performance contribution. (Who wouldn't like to volunteer as a subject for the first experimental application of the cognitive dissonance theory?)

Evaluating the Benchmark Positions

Our compensation structure has now been developed, so we can move on to the placement within this structure of the benchmark positions. The task is basically simple: Each position is placed in the compensation grade whose total compensation control point closely approximates the going rate of total compensation for that position.

Two points should be made here. First, the placement of positions into the structure theoretically could be accomplished either on a base salary control point basis or on a total compensation control point basis. Remember, however, that the distance between the base salary and total compensation control points was established through the use of a normalized bonus curve. Therefore, it is possible that the total compensation control point on certain positions would deviate from the going rate of total compensation as established by the survey, if the base salary control point were used for evaluation. Of course, the reverse can also occur, but it is of less significance because, by using the total compensation control point for evaluation, the company is assured that at least in this most important facet of compensation it is fully competitive.

Second, the question arises as to what to do when the competitor's going rate of total compensation lies between two total compensation control points. One approach is simply to round off—up or down as the case may be. In practice, however, some judgment and a good deal of negotiation will be required. More often than not, most positions will be rounded off to the next *highest* grade. Since the distance between one control point and another is never very great, however, this should not present any real problems.

Slotting the Nonbenchmark Positions

The last remaining task in developing the compensation structure is the evaluation of the nonbenchmark positions. Here is where the management gets deeply involved. And here is where the marketplace method of position evaluation pays off in terms of acceptance by line management.

Although some compensation experts will take issue, the supervisor of a position being considered for evaluation knows more about that position than anyone in personnel. Therefore, the task is to display the benchmark positions in chart form and enter into negotiations with line management on the slotting of the nonbenchmark positions. The word "negotiation" is not used carelessly, for that is ultimately what the slotting process involves. The compensation head does not merely write orders, but then again he is not a judge and jury either. The same applies to the line managers on the other side of the table.

With the chart there for everyone to see, one nonbenchmark position at a time is considered for evaluation. The position is viewed as a whole (taking all its duties and responsibilities together) and is compared to the applicable benchmark positions. Since these positions, if they have been selected properly, cover the entire spectrum of the positions to be evaluated—both vertically and horizontally—the process is essentially one of interpolation and fortunately not of extrapolation. Thus, after some discussion, agreement will usually be reached to the effect that a nonbenchmark position, in terms of duties and responsibilities, lies somewhere between two benchmark positions. After some further discussion and "fine-tuning," the proper grade is finally determined.

This process sounds and *is* rather unscientific. As the president of one firm put it, "All systems of position evaluation essentially boil down to organized rationalization." Remember that the point-factor method, for all its supposed accuracy, is just as unscientific and is also fraught with other problems that have already been discussed.

One helpful technique has been to portray the benchmark positions spatially but without the actual compensation ranges showing. When a line manager can see the ranges, his judgment as to the location of a nonbenchmark position is often clouded by his desire to see that the compensation of the current incumbent doesn't end up above the range maximum.

After the slotting process has been completed and all departments and divisions have had their "day in court," the last step is for the president (or the head of the particular unit) to review the entire structure, looking across disciplinary and divisional lines to insure that equity has been achieved both horizontally and vertically. As a result, some additional fine-tuning may occur, and certain positions may be raised or lowered one grade to conform with the evaluations assigned to comparable positions in different departments or divisions.

Adjusting the Structure

We now have what we know to be a viable compensation structure, one which by definition is externally competitive and, through the nonbenchmark slotting process, is internally equitable. But unless the structure is adjusted periodically, it will soon lose its competitive edge.

How often should the structure be adjusted? Certainly not more than once a year (unless our inflation rate approaches that of Brazil).

In addressing the problem of compensation structure escalation, a company using the marketplace method of position evaluation should adopt a conservative stance, recognizing that the market worth of certain positions moves at a faster rate than others (for example, EDP personnel).

The first step is to ascertain what the trend has been in executive salary escalation over the past year. Here is where published survey data can be of help, by enabling the company to see what several thousand companies have done as well as what the year-to-year trend is by industry. Sources could include AMA's Executive Compensation Service, occasional reports in the business press (such as the ones offered by *Business Week* each year), and data published by the Bureau of Labor Statistics (although these are mainly concerned with the salaries of lower-level personnel and thus will be of only indirect assistance). Still other sources include private surveys in which the firm has participated.

If all these sources make it apparent that executive salaries have increased approximately 4 to 5 percent during the year, the conservative company could then decide to escalate all five points in each range by 4 percent.

Next, the company must determine whether the going rates for any specific positions have moved at a significantly faster pace than 4 percent. Suppose there is good evidence that the market worth of the EDP executive's position has increased 8 percent during the past year. The company should then increase the current base salary control point of this executive's position by 8 percent (before adjusting for the 4 percent general escalation factor). This figure is then compared to the new base salary control points after the overall adjustment of 4 percent has been applied. If, on this basis, a one-grade increase appears desirable, such a course of action could be taken. And if it were taken, those nonbenchmark positions anchored to the EDP executive's position would also be considered for possible reevaluation.

Suppose that the increase in the EDP executive's going rate is not sufficient to justify a one-grade increase at this time. A record should then be kept of the proper new going rate; and next year, if the market worth for this position continues to increase at a faster pace than for other positions, the new escalation percentage could be applied to last year's proper going rate to determine whether a one-grade increase should finally be made.

Adopting a conservative stance in structure escalation eliminates the necessity of downgrading positions.

After adjusting the structure and acting on any market worth anomalies caused by shifting supply and demand, the company should also consider whether certain positions should be upgraded (or downgraded) because they have undergone a significant change in position scope. For example, suppose two divisions have been consolidated into one and the position scope of the division manager, measured in terms of division sales, has increased from $100 million to $200 million. A recheck of the position scope graphs prepared earlier will determine how much of a reevaluation is required to reflect a change of this magnitude.

Because this method of compensation structure escalation is based on industry trend information, it is of course subject to error. Therefore, a periodic resurvey of some, if not all, of the original benchmark positions should be made and the structure adjusted to reflect current trends. In this manner, errors stemming from the use of trend information, which will be small in any event, can be corrected before they are compounded. A resurvey of this type should be undertaken every other year—or at a minimum, every third year.

By following the procedure just mentioned, a company will be assured that its compensation structure is up to date—at least as of the date the revisions are made. Of course, as the months roll by the structure may fall below the market. As a result, some companies add enough additional escalation to the structure to make it theoretically competitive in the middle of the year for which it will be effective, rather than at the beginning of the year. In this manner, the structure will lead the market slightly during the first six months and lag behind slightly during the last six months. There is nothing wrong with such an approach, because it inflates the structure only by one-half year's escalation—or perhaps 2 to 3 percent. Because it is so harmless, however, many other companies will say, "Why bother?" And there is nothing wrong with not bothering either.

★   ★   ★

Although much material has been discussed in this chapter, it all boils down to just a few basic points.

1. Use the marketplace method of position evaluation to save time, properly track the competition, and achieve the needed degree of internal equity.
2. Develop an integrated compensation structure which combines both base salary and total cash compensation progression.
3. Adopt compensation structure escalation procedures which insure that the structure continues to maintain the same competitiveness it had on the day it was first implemented.

3

Executive Performance Appraisal

TODAY a number of new, underdeveloped countries are going in for what is called showcase industrialization. As everyone knows, no country can truly call itself modern unless it is able to manufacture its own automobiles. Thus the first thing that some of these new countries do is build an automobile assembly plant. They quickly discover that they have no one able to design and build the new plant. But no matter; such talent can be imported. After the plant is built, less easily solvable problems arise. For instance, the country's citizens don't possess the education and experience to man the new plant; importing talent this time just won't work. Or there isn't enough electric generating capacity to keep the machines running reliably. Or there are not enough gasoline stations and other service facilities to keep the new cars running. Finally, there aren't more than 50 miles of good road in the whole country!

Thus, before an automobile assembly plant makes economic sense, a host of supporting facilities and services must be in place and operating. In the world of economics, these have been lumped together under the term "infrastructure."

Just as a modern economy requires the proper infrastructure to support it, so does a modern compensation system: In this case, the infrastructure is performance appraisal. Obviously, performance will never be compensated fairly unless it is appraised fairly.

Like its economic counterpart, the performance appraisal infrastructure must vary according to the demands placed upon it. Just as it takes more of an infrastructure to support an automobile assembly plant than a garment factory, so it takes more of a performance appraisal infrastructure to justify bonuses which range from zero to 100 percent of salary than to justify merit increases which range from 3 to 6 percent of salary.

Regrettably, too many top executives are so enamored of the glories of capital gains taxation and the possibilities of income deferrals that they overlook the homely but all-important virtues of a valid performance appraisal system. They pay lip service to performance appraisal, however, and are usually quite willing to adopt any new scheme that comes along so long as it doesn't interfere with getting the "real" job done.

Trait Rating

Until recently, most performance appraisals were of the so-called trait-rating variety, which involved the inference of performance from the measurement of a number of behavioral and personal characteristics. Traits like initiative, reliability, judgment, personality, maturity—even appearance—had a high degree of what the psychologists term face validity. That is, any fool could plainly see that the presence or absence of these traits caused performance to be good or bad. They were in effect the input that led to the performance output.

Unfortunately, however, the correlation between input and output was often dismally low. For all his initiative, maturity, and good looks, the individual somehow failed to achieve good profits for the year. On the other hand, the slob who wore tan shoes with a black suit and kept asking embarrassing questions unaccountably managed to do a great job—despite his characteristics.

Small wonder that most executives turn a deaf ear when their own "traits" are being reviewed and wait as patiently as they can to find out what sort of increase they are getting. About the only sign of life one encounters in these review sessions is when the boss indicates that one of the executive's traits is decidedly negative. "What," the executive then demands to know, "has my 'overly harsh personality' got to do with it? I still managed to beat everyone else's performance, didn't I?" Indeed, one study showed that as the number of negative ratings increased arithmetically, the employee's defensiveness and hostility rose geometrically. Under these circumstances it is unlikely that the employee really absorbs anything that can later be used to improve his performance.

When faced with the irrelevance of traits in rating performance, many companies abandoned the process altogether and fell back on the overall performance rating. Somehow, almost mystically, the individual executive came to be characterized as outstanding, above average, average, and so on. This rating then led to a specific salary increase or bonus action. (Sometimes the salary or bonus action was predetermined and in effect led to a given performance rating.)

These out-of-the-blue overall performance ratings were particularly prone to distortion—especially of the halo and central tendency variety. Thus the rater unconsciously allowed one often insignificant trait to cloud his judgment. A pleasing personality, demonstrated most vividly by a willingness to let the boss win every golf match, could very often offset poor performance in such mundane areas as sales and profits.

In other rating situations, the rater—again unconsciously —would end up giving almost all his subordinates the same rating. And rarely was this single rating on the wrong side of average. For example, in one company 5,000 performance ratings of exempt personnel were distributed in the following manner: outstanding, 30 percent; above average, 40 percent; average, 29 percent; below average, 1 percent.

Just for the fun of it, let us consider the performance reviews where a below average rating has been assigned. Poor performance, at least in this company, was always caused by factors outside the control of the individual. Thus the employee had serious illness in his family; or the job was new to him and he was therefore not yet up to speed. Nowhere in a group of 5,000 employees was a case of good, old-fashioned incompetence to be found. In fact, the rating pattern indicated that the average employee in this company was making performance contributions deemed to be somewhere between above average and outstanding. The only problem was that this conclusion was not supported by the company's profit and loss statement and balance sheet.

Everyone in executive ranks understands the statistical concept of average, but no one wants to be considered average. As a result, the whole rating process has been skewed right, as the statisticians say. To be rated below average nowadays is therefore tantamount to discharge; an average rating is very close to being an insult.

This pattern of glorified performance ratings has led some executives to doubt the validity of their whole performance appraisal system. In some instances, changes for the better have been made. In other cases, however, a company that always prided itself on rewarding performance has promulgated a rather ironic policy to the effect that performance ratings will no longer be used to justify merit increases.

Management by Objectives to the Rescue

A new approach to performance was desperately needed; certainly something had to be done about the morass of invalid ratings, employee resistance, and management disillusionment connected with the present process. A new idea simultaneously occurred to a number of people. Its basic premise was simple and apparently flawless. If the correlation between input and output was not very good, why not eliminate the middleman and measure output directly? Soon a name was coined for this new process: management by objectives.

In its simplest form, management by objectives calls for

the establishment of specific goals, tasks, or objectives (there appears to be little distinction among these three terms so often used) for each executive and the subsequent measurement of whether the executive attained, exceeded, or fell short of his assigned objectives.

Besides being simple and aimed at measuring output rather than input, management by objectives also promises other advantages.

* It gives top management the comforting feeling that everyone knows what he is supposed to do and that he is pulling in the same direction as the rest of the management team.
* It is far more acceptable to the individual executive than the old trait-rating system. At last he can see some rational basis for deciding whether he is great, lousy, or plain average.
* Where he can participate in setting his own goals, the new approach is that much more appealing to the individual executive. Presumably, an individual will work harder when he knows that his target is indeed attainable and realistic.

The ink was barely dry on the first management-by-objectives system when its designer rushed to the nearest meeting of performance appraisal professionals and "told all." His audience, not to be outdone, introduced the system into their own companies. And, shortly, management by objectives came to be thought of as the ultimate in performance assessment systems. Indeed, a progressive company with a system other than management by objectives rapidly became a contradiction in terms.

Yet, despite its initial promise, management by objectives has failed in many companies. Disillusionment is once again rampant. At least five factors seem to be responsible for this development.

Determining the Objectives

First, there is the problem of deciding just what objectives to measure. While some companies have correctly tried to pick objectives which reflect the raison d'être of the position itself, others have persisted in confining objectives to special, one-shot projects. This has been particularly true of staff positions. Thus the controller is not measured on his ability to turn out accurate and timely financial reports but on whether he develops simplified task input worksheets for the factory. This does not necessarily imply that special projects are unimportant, but only indicates that they represent the tip of the iceberg. Simply because the bulk of an executive's job consists of discharging the same responsibilities year in and year out doesn't make these responsibilities any less vital or any less worthy of a prime spot in the executive's objectives for the forthcoming year.

There is also the very real problem of measuring the executive's actual performance against whatever objectives have been selected. This problem is easily resolved, however, by selecting only those objectives which can be readily measured. And that is exactly what many companies do. Thus quantitative objectives, to which numbers can be assigned, are given automatic preference over qualitative objectives, which require a certain amount of judgment to measure. Some quantitative objectives, such as sales and profits, are undoubtedly vital. Some qualitative objectives are equally vital, however. These include the proper selection and development of management talent, the design and implementation of valid management control systems, and the like. But because they cannot be easily measured, they are more than likely to be excluded from the executive's assigned objectives for the year.

In effect, many managers would rather precisely measure their subordinates' progress toward minor objectives than measure as best they can their progress toward major objectives. Yet these same managers accept with equanimity the necessity of being subjective in other areas of management decision making and in their everyday lives. Most of us never get close enough to the girls we see walking down the street to "quantify" them, but that doesn't stop us from doing the very best we can in assessing their important characteristics—and estimating their probable performance.

Unfortunately, objectives that can be easily quantified are generally short term, and thus the individual's orientation at any point in time is also likely to be short term. Since most people are more comfortable with short-term goals anyway, no one is likely to be particularly unhappy over this turn of events. However, an overemphasis on short-term accomplishments, such as the maximization of sales and profits, without due regard for longer-term considerations, such as research and development and proper selection and training, can lead to brilliance one year and bankruptcy the next.

As much as many of us would like to confine our efforts to tasks which are easily measurable and can be fully completed this year, the fact is that today's increasingly sophisticated technology won't permit us this luxury.

The length of time between inception of an idea and its ultimate fruition is growing inexorably. If management by objectives is to work well, it must reflect, not fight, this trend.

Weighting the Objectives

Second is the problem of assessing the importance of each objective. Obviously, each of the five or so objectives assigned to an executive will vary in importance to the company. Yet there seems to be no easy way to assign tangible weights to the objectives. In its extreme forms, this difficulty leads to two divergent approaches to assessment—both of them wrong. If, for example, the executive has met or exceeded four of his five objectives, someone is likely to overlook a failure on the last (after all, no one is perfect!), even though it was the profit objective.

The reverse can also occur. The executive achieves his sales and profit goals but fails on the other three objectives. His seeming ineptness is overlooked, because "sales and profits are really the only things that count. The rest of the objectives are merely icing on the cake." Thus rationalization, that favorite device of thinking people everywhere, makes management by objectives look like management by subjectives.

Rating the Objectives

Third is the problem of rating each objective. Most previous rating systems were predicated on the industrial engineering approach to work measurement. Thus a standard was established to represent the amount of work that the "average" worker could reasonably be expected to produce. But executive objectives, like corporate objectives, are set to encourage more than simply average performance. Unfortunately, the amount of "stretch" varies from objective to objective and from person to person. Attaining the sales objective, for example, might represent truly superlative performance; yet attaining the profit objective might represent little more than average performance. Similarly, the fact that two executives meet their objectives does not necessarily mean that the performance of the two men is equal.

To combat this problem, some companies established objectives with reference to past accomplishments. Who could argue that a 25 percent increase in sales this year as compared to last year did not connote truly outstanding performance? Unhappily, however, this approach led to two other problems.

1. If market conditions the next year cause a reversal from a buyer's to a seller's market, the manager could achieve the 25 percent increase if he were to stay home in bed for all but one week of the year. (The opposite could also occur, such that barely staying even with last year's results would require performance that is really extraordinary.)

2. Although two executives have the same objective of improving sales by 25 percent, one finds his objective a lot easier to accomplish than the other because his sales last year (upon which this year's objective is based) were substantially below the industry average. After all, it is easier to reach the average from a below average position than to achieve outstanding performance from an above average position.

Gamesmanship

Fourth, there has been a good deal of gamesmanship evidenced in the objective-setting process. Recognizing that the basis of their compensation (as well as promotion) is the attainment of their objectives, many executives do their best to keep their objectives as low as possible. Since few people take the time to determine the degree of stretch that is going into each objective, one is sure to receive more "points" for surpassing what are in reality easy objectives than for falling just short of what are in reality brutally tough objectives. The atmosphere in objective-setting sessions, then, is not unlike that in collective bargaining sessions. One unfortunate result is that some executives end up with an easier set of objectives than do other executives. Just because they are better bargainers, however, doesn't necessarily mean that they are also better performers.

Taking the Time Required

Fifth and finally, there is the problem of time. Because it looks so simple, many executives think that management by objectives requires little of their time. They are wrong. Management by objectives is a time-consuming process. Time must be spent in determining the types of objectives to be established. Time must be spent in building the proper degree of stretch into each objective. And time must be spent in assessing performance against objectives at the end of the year. Managers who think management by objectives is more accurate and quicker have learned that, in the business of performance appraisal, accuracy and speed are mutually exclusive.

Do all these problems mean that management by objectives, a relatively new system, is already moribund? No. The concept of measuring output rather than input is still—and always will be—viable. The execution of the concept is another matter, however, and certain steps can be taken to resolve some of these problems.

Determining the Types of Objectives

First, let us examine the problem of deciding which objectives to include. Obviously not all the executive's objectives can be included for performance measurement or the list would be too unwieldy. On the other hand, the list of objectives should not be confined merely to special projects. It should embrace and represent the totality of the executive's duties and responsibilities. And it should include not only objectives which can be fully completed during the year but also milestones toward the accomplishment of longer-range or infinitely continuing objectives upon which the business depends for its future growth and profitability. Many of these latter objectives are necessarily qualitative in nature and therefore difficult to measure, but handling messy situations is presumably why managers earn a lot of money.

For example, let us assume that a division manager is going to be assigned the following five types of objectives for the forthcoming year: (1) sales; (2) profits; (3) development of a management information system; (4) research and development; and (5) development of new executives. These are not yet objectives since the amount of performance to be required in each area has not been specified. They are, however, steps on the way to determining objectives.

Weighting the Objectives

Once the types of objectives to be utilized are developed, the relative importance of each should be assessed, since it is unlikely that all are of equal importance. To aid in this process, we can borrow a technique utilized by statisticians in developing indexes such as the Consumer Price Index. First, we assume that, in total, all five types of objectives equal 100 percent. Dividing 100 percent by five in turn produces an average weighting of 20 percent per objective. This is the implicit weight that would be assigned were it concluded that each objective was equal in importance to every other objective.

In our illustration, however, we assume that such is not the case and that the sales and profit objectives are necessarily more important than the remaining three, so we increase the percentage weightings to be applied to these objectives. Since the sum of all objective weights must always equal 100 percent, we have to decrease the weight on certain other objectives. Suppose we decide that the development of a management information system and the development of new executives, although important (or they wouldn't have been included), are the least important. A possible weighting pattern appears on the next page.

It should be obvious at this point that the process of weighting objectives cannot be scientifically precise and can contain some degree of standard error. Thus the sales goal, which has been given a 30 percent weighting, could just as easily have been given a weighting of 25 or 35 per-

101

Type of Objective	Weighting (Percent)
1. Sales	30
2. Profits	35
3. Development of management in- formation system	10
4. Research and development	20
5. Development of new executives	5
Total	100

cent. On the other hand, it would be unlikely for the correct sales goal weighting to be as low as 15 percent or as high as 45 percent. Weightings, then, help to establish orders of magnitude. And, as is demonstrated shortly, minor errors in weighting are unlikely to have any significant influence on the final performance appraisal results.

Adding the Performance "Stretch"

The third step, after determining the types of objectives to be utilized and assigning them weights, is to complete the objective-setting process by adding specific performance targets to each objective. In so doing, the amount of performance implied in the attainment of each objective—that is, the stretch—should be the same for each objective and the same for each executive. Essentially, two approaches can be used:

1. Establish each objective so that its accomplishment represents average performance.
2. Establish each objective so that its accomplishment represents outstanding performance.

The first approach seems the most appealing because it conforms with previously used industrial engineering-oriented approaches to work measurement and performance appraisal. When it comes to executive performance appraisal, however, there is often considerable disagreement as to just what constitutes average performance; hence gamesmanship in setting objectives is more prevalent. Moreover, some experts feel that establishing more demanding objectives causes executives to increase their efforts so that they can achieve the psychological satisfaction that comes from their success and conversely to avoid the psychological dissonance that stems from their falling short. (On the other hand, it could be argued that giving the executive a better chance of exceeding his objectives through the use of average performance standards might be a psychologically better approach.)

The second approach—establishing each objective so that its accomplishment represents outstanding performance—seems, on balance, to be more desirable. Although the exact point at which performance is considered average is difficult to discern, there appears to be less difficulty in spotting outstanding performance. As with most things, the extremes are always more visible than the average. This approach may also motivate increased executive effort.

As an illustration, let us adopt the second alternative and establish each objective so that its attainment represents outstanding performance—which is likely to be achieved by only 10 to 15 percent of all executives (that is, the 85th to 90th percentile of accomplishment). The five types of objectives might then look like this:

1. Achieve sales of $100 million.
2. Achieve pretax profits of $20 million.

3. Develop all basic parameters of a potential new management information system and perform cost-benefit analyses.
4. Develop, and prepare for production next year, new products with a potential first-year sales volume of $25 million.
5. Develop qualified replacements for five key positions.

Rating Performance Against Objectives

The next step is to develop a numerical rating scheme to be used in evaluating actual performance against preestablished objectives. Any number of alternative schemes can be adopted, but for illustrative purposes, let us use the following one:

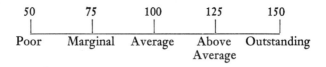

Whatever rating scheme is adopted, it should, like this one, be symmetrical and contain just as much room below the average as above. The scheme used by some restaurants ("How did you like the service? Outstanding? Excellent? Good?") simply will not do. As a matter of convenience, it is also desirable to establish the numerical rating for average performance as 100; the reasons are given shortly.

Since each of the objectives in our illustration has been established to represent outstanding performance, it follows that each, if attained, will receive a rating of 150 points. Where actual performance falls short of the objective, the rating would of course be less than 150 points and could be as low as 50 points. It is also possible that performance could exceed the goal. Such an event is unlikely to occur, however, because, as noted earlier, the objective has been established with only a 10 to 15 percent probability of accomplishment. Nevertheless, performance which is *significantly* above the goal should in all fairness be recognized, and, although the rating scheme shown here stops at 150 points, there is no reason why it can't be extended to accommodate exceptional cases. (From a symmetry standpoint, the bottom end of the rating scheme must also be extended, although from a practical standpoint the chances of its being used are infinitesimal considering the pronounced tendency to overrate most personnel.)

To maximize motivation, it would be highly desirable if, after establishing each 150-point objective, we could indicate in advance what rating would accrue to various levels of performance which fell short of the goal. Although such an approach is well-nigh impossible in the case of essentially qualitative goals (such as the last three in our illustration), it can be readily adopted for quantitative goals such as sales and profits. In effect, subsidiary schedules for each of these quantitative goals should be established to show the points that will be given for various levels of achievement. These schedules should be built around an acceleration principle, such that the closer the performance approaches the goal, the faster the accumulation of points. This principle underscores that it is harder to improve by, say, 10 percent when performance is already excellent than it is to make the same percentage improvement when the current performance level is below average.

For illustrative purposes, let us assume that, although

$100 million in sales represents outstanding performance
and carries with it a 150-point rating, $75 million in sales
represents performance which is just short of intolerable.
A subsidiary point schedule might then look like this:

Sales Performance (Millions)	Point Rating
$100	150
95	112
90	87
85	70
80	58
75	50

It can be seen in this example that the number of points
accelerates sharply as performance approaches the goal. For
example, an increase in sales from $75 million to $80 million
carries with it a 16 percent increase in rating—or eight
points. On the other hand, an increase in sales from $95
million to $100 million carries with it a 34 percent increase
in rating—or 38 points.

Determining the Overall Performance Rating

At the end of the year, after the actual performance
against each objective has been assessed and a numerical rating assigned, an overall performance rating can be established in a very simple manner. All that need be done is to
multiply the weighting on each objective by the rating assigned to that objective, add up the resulting figures, and
divide by 100. This process can be demonstrated using our
illustration once again and assuming that certain performance levels have occurred.

Objective	Weighting	Rating	Weighting × Rating (Percent)
1. Sales of $100 million	30	135	4,050
2. Profits of $20 million	35	115	4,025
3. Management information system	10	75	750
4. Research and development	20	100	2,000
5. Development of new executives	5	50	250
Totals	100		11,075

Overall rating: 11,075/100 = 111

The overall rating of 111 points is assessed with reference to the same scale used to establish the rating for each of the individual objectives. Thus 111 points represent overall performance which is about halfway between average and above average.

At this point, the process just described may be questioned on at least two counts. First, one could say that the approach is overly mechanistic and lends an unfounded aura of scientific accuracy to what must always be essentially a subjective, judgmental process. This criticism is warranted if one assumes that great significance ought to be attached to the difference between a rating of 111 points and ratings of 110 and 112 points. However, as in any measuring system of this type (and that includes such presumably incontrovertible statistics as the Consumer Price Index), there is always some degree of standard error. In this particular case, the standard error could run as high as 10 points on either side of any rating derived. Thus the rating of 111 points in our example might well have turned out to be as low as 101 points or as high as 121 points—the entire range of 20 points would be treated as if it were a single rating. On the other hand, significance could—and should—be attached to ratings as divergent as 100 points and 130 points.

The suggested performance appraisal system in no way substitutes for judgment; it merely assists what is ultimately a judgmental process by breaking down one huge judgment (overall performance) into a number of smaller, more manageable judgments.

A second criticism may be that the suggested system allows anyone with even the slightest intelligence to "fudge" and in essence dream up weightings and ratings to fit a predetermined conclusion as to the overall performance rating. There is no doubt that some will try to do just this. But the individual who tries to foil this system can be counted on to make the same attempt with any other system. One of the safeguards that this system has over others, however, is its ability to make explicit all the assumptions leading to an overall performance assessment that in other systems are always implicit and impossible to check.

Another safeguard is a fairly strong central tendency which is built into the system. Say we want to change a rating from 110 points to 130 points (remember that there is probably a 10-point standard error in the system, and changes of this magnitude don't count anyway). To make this change will require either a tremendous reweighting, involving the assignment of almost all the weight on those objectives which carry the highest ratings (and this is unlikely because weights are assigned in advance); or a tremendous rerating of the performance points on all or a number of objectives (and this is partially controlled by preestablished subsidiary point schedules for quantitative objectives); or a combination of both reweighting and rerating. To achieve a truly significant increase in the overall point rating, therefore, the rater runs the real risk of assigning transparently phony weights and ratings, all of which are subject to review by his superiors.

The system of performance appraisal suggested in this chapter is not easy. It will take a considerable amount of time if the job is to be done right. And it will still require the guts to make rather dirty, subjective decisions. But the job is well worth doing. Without the infrastructure of valid performance assessment, the remainder of compensation planning becomes a travesty.

4

Paying for Performance

THE compensation structure in its totality may be viewed as a giant plus sign. An individual executive moves up the vertical bar of the plus sign (from one control point to another) in accordance with the responsibilities assigned him. He moves across the horizontal bar of the plus sign (from base salary minimum to total compensation maximum) in accordance with his performance. We now turn our attention to the movement along the horizontal bar.

Making Use of the Learning Curve

Many companies have contented themselves with rather simple rules for determining the size of an increase an executive is to receive. As one company put it, "We give

110

10 percent for outstanding performance, 8 percent for above average performance, 6 percent for average performance and nothing for below average performance."

Such an approach neglects two very important factors. First, the progress of human learning is very uneven. Repeated psychological studies have demonstrated that all human learning—and increased performance on the job is essentially a matter of learning—follows a similar pattern: One learns a given task extremely rapidly at first and then begins to slow down over a period of time. Eventually, the rate of learning peaks out and may even decline in some instances. Now, when one thinks about it, the way in which people learn is really rather logical, since if one doesn't know much to begin with, it is fairly easy to double one's knowledge in a short period of time. On the other hand, if one already knows a great deal, it takes much longer to double one's knowledge.

If compensation is going to be used as a motivational tool, it must match the individual's performance. Since not all individuals perform in the same manner, matching compensation to performance means that some will get a lot more than others. Hence we have the basis for recognition. And it is recognition, especially at the executive level, that is highly motivating.

If compensation is going to match performance, then it obviously must match the learning curve. Unfortunately, however, too many companies fail to follow this principle. If an executive's performance is improving rapidly because he is on a new job and hence on the steep portion of his learning curve, he is still likely to get only a 10 percent increase at most. Later, when his performance has slowed down but is on a sustained high level, the 10 percent increase will still be coming along as regular as clockwork.

In a way, the compensation practices at these companies are comparable to an old cargo ship pulling out of New York harbor: The pace is terribly slow at first and not much faster later on, but eventually it gets you there. The trouble is that this approach opens a terrible compensation gap during the years when the individual is on the steep portion of his learning curve. He is moving at jet speed, while the company's compensation program chugs along at 15 knots. This gap is illustrated in Exhibit 3, wherein a typical company compensation curve is superimposed on the learning curve.

It is noted in this exhibit that the typical company com-

Exhibit 3 **Typical compensation progression versus typical learning curve.**

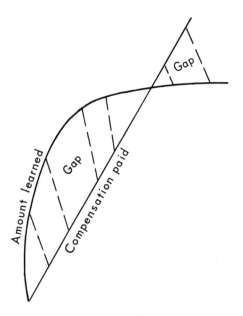

pensation curve eventually crosses the learning curve, thereby creating a gap in the opposite direction. Obviously this doesn't happen in every case but the high incidence of overpaid executives is nonetheless discomforting. "I just can't understand how that guy can make so much money," is a comment often heard in company corridors. Indeed, the problem is such that it has been facetiously suggested more than once that the company should at least capitalize on its policies by telling its executives, "Stick with us long enough, and on the average, you'll receive the proper amount of compensation during your career with the company."

In today's highly competitive environment for executive talent, however, this is no solution. Those whom the company most wants to keep are the very ones who are likely to be lost unless the compensation gap is closed. This happens because the steeper the learning curve, the better the performance and potential of the individual; and the steeper the learning curve, the wider the compensation gap is likely to be.

Establishing Compensation Targets for
Varying Performance Levels

A second and related problem with the approach of granting a given percentage of increase for a given performance level is that it fails to take into account the individual's current compensation position. Thus a man who is outstanding but whose earnings are only average will most likely receive the same 10 percent increase as the man who is outstanding but who is already earning an outstanding salary. In fact, the problem will be exacerbated because the percentage is applied to a much lower salary in the case of the first individual.

The proper amount of compensation increase, then, should be determined by the gap between where the individual is now and where he should be according to his performance contributions.

The concept is simple, but many companies consistently fail to apply it. In effect, it's as if a company's top executives and those whose compensation is being controlled are speaking two different languages. On the one hand, the top management, in response to compensation complaints, says, "What does the guy want? He's had two promotions in the past two years and we've given him the 10 percent maximum merit increase for as long as we can remember. He's come a long way fast, and he ought to be satisfied." The complaining manager, on the other hand, says, "I know I've come a long way fast, but I'm still way behind where I should be in terms of what I am supposed to do and the manner in which I'm doing it."

In a way, both these points of view are correct, but equity is on the side of the manager whose compensation is lagging behind his performance.

Such gaps can be closed by a simple stroke of the pen—certainly with much less trouble than the resolution of a personality conflict or some other intangible problem. Yet they continue to remain open. Top managers of companies with these problems are usually very pragmatic when it comes to negotiating with unions, because they really have no choice. And they are pragmatic when it comes to negotiating with a prospective executive who is employed by another company. Unless a satisfactory compensation package is offered, the executive will simply stay where he is or seek employment elsewhere. Yet once an individual joins the company and is not represented by a union, the top managers, for some inexplicable reason, assume that the rules of the marketplace do not apply. If a compensation problem develops, given enough time, they will solve it. More likely, one of their competitors will solve it for them.

Another irritating practice is to recognize the gap concept and the gap itself but refuse to do anything about it on the grounds that a big increase will spoil an executive and make him want the same treatment every year. Certainly the executive may want the same treatment every year—who wouldn't? But presumably he didn't get where he is without a certain degree of maturity, and therefore he should be capable of realizing that he can't remain on a steep learning curve forever. (A baby weighing 8 pounds at birth who continued gaining at his initial rate by doubling his weight every six months would weigh some 263 tons by the time he was eight years old!) There is far less risk in paying each executive what he is worth when he is worth it and taking the chance of having a few malcontents than in following the reverse procedure and insuring that there will be many malcontents—all excellent performers.

The proper and more motivationally rewarding policy that a company should follow is to establish targeted positions within the compensation range for various levels of performance. Since the base salary control point and the total compensation control point have been set to equal competitors' going rates, it follows that these are the targeted points for the average performer (that is, one with a performance point rating of 90 to 110). Other targeted positions would include—

* *Base salary minimum and no bonus* for the new executive who is still not up to speed or for the poor performer (performance point rating of 50 to 70).

* *Halfway between the base salary minimum and control points and no bonus* for the mediocre to marginal executive (performance point rating of 70 to 90).

* *A combination of salary and bonus equal to an amount halfway between the total compensation control and maximum points* for the above average executive (performance point rating of 110 to 130).

* *A combination of salary and bonus equal to an amount ranging up to the maximum total compensation point* for the truly outstanding performer (performance point rating of 130 to 150).

Once these targeted positions are established, the merit increase is determined by computing the gap between the point in the range that the executive now occupies and the point he should occupy according to his performance assessment.

Closing Compensation Gaps

Theoretically, all gaps, no matter how large, should be closed at once. From a practical standpoint, however, a company may wish to use some prudence. For example, gaps of 15 percent or less could be closed at once, and those of more than 15 percent could be closed in a series of more frequent but smaller increases, such that the gap becomes fully closed within a period of two years at the outside. Meanwhile, the bonus can be used to take up the slack.

Closing a compensation gap, however, requires the same ability to track the target as does shooting a duck, for a compensation gap is unlikely to remain static. First, the individual may still be improving his performance in his current position; thus, if his targeted position today is based on an assessment as an above average performer, it may well be based next year on an assessment as an outstanding performer.

Second, the range itself is escalating from year to year owing to such factors as productivity and cost of living.

Third, the individual may well be promoted very soon. So, although his targeted performance position is lower, he is in a higher range, thereby causing his dollar target to rise significantly.

Fourth, the individual may succeed in increasing the scope of the present position, thereby causing a reevaluation of the position and possibly a classification in a higher compensation grade. The result is identical to that of a bona fide promotion.

Thus, if the individual's current compensation gap is 20 percent, it may not remain so for long, and the company had better plan a string of, say, 15 percent increases to be granted at six-month intervals to insure that its tracking is correct and that the gap will be closed in the maximum two-year period.

Using Potential as a Compensation Factor

Looked at another way, the problem of tracking a moving gap is really one of estimating an executive's potential for future growth. Now, some will say that potential has no business being in a compensation program and that only current demonstrated performance should count. This is similar to saying that one can drive at 90 miles per hour whether the distance is 100 feet or 100 miles. To reassure the purists, the use of an executive's potential for tracking purposes in no way causes him to be overpaid at any time in terms of his current demonstrated performance. All that happens is that the current gap, which has nothing whatever to do with a man's potential, is closed at a faster rate if it is believed that future performance or position growth will not be long in coming.

Incorporating the concept of potential into the compensation system requires some care, however. To say that a man has potential is utterly devoid of meaning unless one knows the answers to two questions: Potential for what? Potential in what period of time? At a given point, an executive's potential to become, say, a vice-president is obviously different from his potential to become president of the company. Moreover, his potential to become a vice-president in one year differs from his potential to make it in two years.

It seems that for compensation tracking purposes the prediction of potential for a period in excess of two years is too risky. Accordingly, the compensation planner should consider an executive's potential within this time frame and for various performance levels or new positions.

Handling Negative Gaps

Sometimes, of course, we are faced with a negative compensation gap, where the individual's current compensation exceeds his targeted range position. Obviously no action should be taken if the gap is small because periodic escalations in the compensation structure will remove the gap in a relatively short time—and because of the factor of standard error in performance appraisal.

On the other hand, large negative gaps (say 15 percent

or more) may require a very unpalatable course of action: a salary decrease. This is especially the case if the company has been following the compensation gap philosophy in the past, because in that event a negative gap would be likely to stem only from a performance decline. In such a situation, the chances of a performance improvement are slim (unless the reasons for the decline are entirely external to the individual), but the chances of further decline are somewhat greater.

Using Compensation Ranges as Guidelines

Some executives react with horror at the thought of anyone's compensation going above the maximum of his range. (Compensation below the minimum is of course an indication of prudent management!) To them, the maximum is not a guideline but a concrete wall. Although their anxiety is understandable (having to abandon the safety of the average is bad enough but going above the maximum is ridiculous), they do their company a disservice by holding to their beliefs. For the maximum—at least as it has been designed in Chapter 2—*is* a guideline.

Remember that the minimum and the maximum range points were established to "cut off the tails" of the curve and eliminate the spurious portions of the frequency distribution. As such, these points represent approximately the 10th to the 90th percentiles of the distribution. Therefore, it is still possible—although admittedly improbable—for an individual to turn in a performance which is so superb as to justify paying him above the maximum of his assigned range. Albert Einstein would probably have qualified for such compensation treatment. Moreover, there is no reason why such an individual should not continue to receive still further increases.

The alternative to such an approach is to reevaluate the man's position and assign it a phony compensation grade. But this alternative may have repercussions on the evaluations of other positions in the organization, thereby increasing the company's potential compensation costs. Furthermore, when the superb performer finally leaves his position, he will probably not be replaced by someone equally superb; yet the unduly high compensation grade will probably not be lowered.

Consider, if you will, that paying compensation above the maximum represents the ultimate in recognition. What better way is there to motivate superb performance?

Timing the Increase

There is considerable disagreement in the compensation field as to when an individual should be reviewed for salary action. Some say annually on the individual's anniversary date (or some other date which staggers reviews throughout the year). Some say annually on a department by department basis. Some say annually for everyone after the close of the year. Although there are pros and cons to each of these approaches, the last one mentioned seems preferable. It ties in with a performance appraisal system geared to the attainment of objectives, which, after all, are usually established on a fiscal-year basis. Having to review the performance of many executives at once can be a drain on the reviewers and may therefore reduce the quality of appraisals, but a review system which randomly staggers increases throughout the year would lose its all-important motivational link with demonstrated performance.

Increases should be considered for times other than the annual review, however. For example, when a large compensation gap cannot be closed all at once, increases at six-month intervals can be usefully employed.

A case can also be made for giving an occasional spot increase to an executive who has demonstrated exceptional skill on a particular project. Such an increase, which would have to operate within the compensation gap principle and not create a negative gap, can be highly motivational simply because it is totally unexpected. Like investors in the stock market, executives anticipate what their regular merit increases will be and then "discount" future growth. When they receive the increase they anticipated, their short-term motivation, like the price of a stock which has already been discounted, may not rise appreciably. On the other hand, an increase at an unexpected time can be enormously stimulating, especially when it comes immediately after the performance on which it is based and therefore increases the cause-and-effect relationship between rewards and performance that is at the motivational heart of any sound compensation program.

There are some companies that slow down the frequency of merit increases as the executive begins to near the maximum. Thus the executive is reviewed annually until he reaches the control point of his range; thereafter the review period is stretched to 18 months until he reaches a point halfway between the control point and the maximum. Then the review period moves to two years. These companies explain their policy through reference to the learning curve. As the individual's performance moves past the average mark his rate of growth necessarily slows down.

On its face, such an explanation makes sense. But these companies seem to want the best of both worlds, since there is little evidence that early salary progression is extremely fast because of the same learning curve principle. Moreover, these companies fail to use potential in tracking the executive's short-term progress over, say, the next two years. Viewed on this basis, the executive may be nowhere near running out of gas.

Slowing down the frequency of merit review is an acceptable—even desirable—policy when an executive shows signs of reaching the end of his *career* learning curve. Short of that, it is more of a disincentive ("congratulations, your performance is outstanding, and as a reward we are going to review you once every two years") and simply leads to the creation of a wider compensation gap.

The real reason why companies slow down the merit increase frequency is to prevent the individual from reaching the maximum and having no further room to move. As noted earlier, it seems far more desirable to work on closing compensation gaps than to worry about the dire motivational consequences that might ensue from paying a man what he is worth.

Publishing the Structure

After developing a viable compensation structure and intelligent rules for its use, the company must then concern itself with the effect the new structure's publication will have on its executives. Some executives balk at publishing their compensation structure and merit review guidelines because they feel it can only cause trouble. First, executives in certain disciplines will come to realize that they don't have as high an earning potential as executives in other disciplines. Second, a man will put great pressure on the company if the rules say an outstanding individual is supposed to be at the maximum and he is outstanding but somewhere lower in his range. Third, there will also be pressure on the company to give everyone an increase at least equal to the amount of the annual structure escalation because not to do so would imply a performance decline under the review guidelines.

Let us consider these objections. First, to think that executives are not aware of interdisciplinary differences in market worth is to give them little credit for knowing what is going on in American business. Second, it is true that a man whose performance is considered outstanding but who is not at the maximum of his range will put pressure on the company to remedy the inequity, but why shouldn't he? Perhaps, by publishing the ranges and the accompanying guidelines, the company in some cases will be forced to call a spade a spade and tell an average executive that he is average, rather than buoy up his morale by giving him a false impression of his performance.

Third, it is also true that by not increasing an individual's salary at the same rate applied to the structure, a performance decline is implied. Yet the performance decline is not necessarily absolute but can be relative to the performance of other executives. Presumably, increases in the compensation structure reflect not only cost-of-living and supply–demand factors but also at least some amount of increased productivity. In the case of an executive, increased productivity doesn't necessarily mean that the job is getting done faster each year. Rather, it usually means that the knowledge and experience required to perform the job are steadily increasing as a function of increasing technology. Witness the computer, which has made the jobs of some managers easier but has greatly complicated the jobs of others—especially top managers. People who couldn't spell "operations research" and "linear programming" yesterday must now be able not only to spell them but to understand them. Thus today's mediocre manager would probably have been considered outstanding a decade or so ago; and today's outstanding manager will probably be considered mediocre in the next decade unless he continues to increase his "productivity."

Thus there is an ever increasing number of executives who, although doing as well as ever, are failing to keep up with the advance in technology and hence are falling behind when compared to their peers. Giving them increases which implicitly deny this fact would seem to be doing them a grave disservice over the long term.

It seems evident that the arguments against publishing the compensation structure and its guidelines are tenuous. On the other hand, there are some compelling arguments *for* publication. The most important is the opportunity that management has to make better use of the recognition principle. A man who reads the published material and observes that he is at the maximum of his range—or even above it—knows that his performance is outstanding and is being recognized. A man who reads the published material and observes that he is at the control point knows—despite the saccharine rhetoric of his boss—that he is only average; he probably knew it anyway. In short, if compensation motivates through recognition, why defeat these motivational purposes by shrouding the company's compensation policies in secrecy?

Publishing the compensation structure and its guidelines also has another salutary effect. It forces management to hew to its own policies. Compensation gaps are likely to be closed more quickly if everyone knows it is supposed to be done. Because of this, and because no company has unlimited funds to spend on increases, the number of individuals not receiving increases is likely to rise. Thus a new kind of compensation gap will be created—between outstanding and mediocre performers. That is the kind of gap that creates recognition and the motivation to achieve the company's corporate objectives.

Promotional Increases

One last item deserving of mention here is promotional increases. For some reason, a number of companies consistently refuse to grant promotional increases at the time of promotion. The increase follows either at the time of the next merit review or when "the man has proved he can do the job." This is a clear-cut violation of the risk versus reward principle. The executive is being asked to take a riskier job; he also must take more personal risks while he is learning how to function in his new position. Moreover, if management didn't already think he would be effective in the new position, it presumably wouldn't have offered him the promotion in the first place.

Increases should, if anything, be greater for promotions than for merit reviews, and they should always occur at the time the promotion is granted. An increase should take the executive at least to the minimum of his new range (no matter what percentage is required), because there is no valid reason for keeping anyone below the minimum. And, if there is reason to believe that the executive's performance will be more than minimal in a short time (say, six months), then he should be taken to the targeted range position applicable to that level of performance.

★   ★   ★

The motivational value of compensation can be increased by paying for performance through—

1. Establishing targeted range positions for various levels of performance.
2. Using an executive's short-term potential to track his anticipated performance and position growth.
3. Adopting the compensation gap principle and a policy which aims at closing current and anticipated gaps as soon as possible after they occur, but within no more than two years.
4. Publishing the compensation structure and its associated guidelines.
5. Granting meaningful increases at the time of the promotion.

5

The Executive Bonus

A company's bonus plan is potentially the single most important motivational element in its entire compensation package. The key word here is "potentially"; unless certain design principles are followed, a bonus plan's potential will never be realized. Although most of these principles have been introduced earlier, it will be well to recapitulate here.

Basic Design Principles

First, the plan must be designed to stimulate behavior which leads to the attainment of the goals the company really wants to attain. We have seen that this design task requires a great deal of thought, because a company's real goals are not always what convention dictates. For example,

127

the maximization of profits in any one year may contain the seeds of great troubles, if not bankruptcy, in future years. This occurs when profits are maximized at the expense of research and development expenditures, investment in modernization of plant and equipment, and proper organizational staffing and development. The fact is that probably no single goal can be used to describe adequately why any company is in business. Even though multiple goals complicate the bonus plan, they must be employed.

Second, the plan should be extended only to those executives whose duties and responsibilities give them the opportunity to make a material and substantial impact (for good or ill) on the achievement of the goals. While it is true that every employee has some impact on the achievement of goals, it is equally true that few employees have a really *substantial* impact. It is these executives to whom the plan must be directed. This is not to say that special awards should not be given to the rare individual in a lower-level position who performs better than was ever expected.

Third, the plan should provide for payment of truly meaningful awards. Awards of one month's salary are ineffective. Bonuses will have to range upward of 50 to 60 percent at the highest levels in order to motivate. Moreover, the bonuses should rise sharply as the company closes on its objectives to recognize that these last increments of performance are the hardest to achieve and at the same time are the most profitable.

Fourth, the plan should distinguish between the performance contributions of individual executives, offering some of them a maximum award and others no award.

Fifth, and finally, the plan will have to be revised and strengthened from time to time to overcome the inevitable erosion that most companies experience.

Eligibility

Determining who is and who is not eligible for the executive bonus plan is without a doubt the dirtiest job in the plan's design. It is easy to say that those whose duties and responsibilities offer them the opportunity to make a substantial impact on the attainment of goals should be eligible. The converse is also true: Those whose duties and responsibilities do not offer them the opportunity to make a substantial impact should be ineligible. But how does one distinguish between substantial and insubstantial impact when the responsibilities in any company are not discrete but overlapping and continuous, extending in an unbroken progression from the janitor to the president?

The fact is that wherever the line is drawn, the result is going to be at least somewhat arbitrary. Some companies have ducked behind titles and said that only officers are eligible to participate. This kind of selection causes a number of "statutory" officers (for example, an assistant secretary) to be included unnecessarily. Some companies have gone to the other extreme and declared that all exempt personnel are eligible, but this is merely ducking behind the Fair Labor Standards Act, in which definitions of exempt and nonexempt personnel are extremely arbitrary.

There is no easy answer, then, to the question of eligibility. But there are certain guidelines to use in this dirty job.

First, a distinction can be drawn between those whose responsibilities cause them to have a two-way impact on the attainment of goals and those whose responsibilities permit them to have only a one-way impact. To illustrate, if the decisions that some executives make turn sour, the result can be harmful to the company. Yet, if those decisions turn out to be wise, the results can be highly beneficial. Thus executives of this type have a two-way impact on the attainment of goals.

On the other hand, take the case of a dispatcher in a pipeline. His is a highly paid job, and he is responsible for the correct and timely movement of millions of gallons of oil products. If he makes the wrong decisions, his products may be contaminated, customers may receive the wrong delivery, or the pipeline may be completely stopped. Thus there is a lot riding on his successful performance. Yet, if this dispatcher makes all the right decisions, the best that can happen is that the company will not suffer. His is a job with only one-way impact. He can foul things up with a vengeance, but he can rarely make the company better than it already is.

There are many people in a company with one-way impact, but there are few with true two-way impact.

Another guideline is the practices of one's competitors, although obviously this should not be followed in a totally mechanistic fashion. Studies have shown that, as a company increases in size, the number of bonus eligibles also increases; however, the number of bonus eligibles as a percentage of the total company population decreases. This is as it should be, for doubling in size does not require doubling the number of key executives. Rather, a limited number of new key executive positions are created, and the current executives receive an increase in their position scope.

Generally speaking, large companies whose employees number 25,000 or more typically extend bonus eligibility to about 1 percent of their total population. Companies in the 5,000 to 25,000 size range usually extend bonus eligibility to 1 to 2 percent of their total population. These figures must be tempered by four considerations, however.

First, the percentage of bonus eligibles is generally higher in labor-intensive industries than in capital-intensive industries. In the latter group, fewer and more major decisions are made, often involving hundreds of millions of dollars at one time, and as a result few executives are entrusted with such decisions.

Second, the percentage of bonus eligibles is higher in companies with sophisticated technology than in companies making fairly mundane products. Although these companies cover about the same percentage of their exempt population as companies with less sophisticated technology, their coverage as a percentage of total population is higher because they have so many more exempt personnel.

Third, the percentage of bonus eligibles in decentralized companies with divisionalized organizational structures is generally higher than that in centralized companies. This is related to the earlier discussion of labor-intensive industries. In both situations, decision making is spread to more executives.

Fourth, the percentage of bonus eligibles is generally higher in the most successful companies than in the least successful companies. One study relating bonus eligibility percentages to returns on assets for 16 companies showed that the correlation was 0.6. Although one might conclude that the most successful companies got that way because they covered more people for bonus eligibility, it is more likely that they were better able to grant more awards.

Ultimately, the question of eligibility levels is decided pragmatically. A company can allocate only so much money to executive bonuses without angering the shareholders. Thus it usually faces a choice of having many eligibles and low awards or few eligibles and very meaningful awards. From a motivational standpoint, of course, there is no choice but the second alternative.

One approach to eligibility determination is to target a percentage of total population using the guidelines just mentioned, select the positions to be included, calculate the funds required, and consider whether the funding formula needed to produce these funds is excessive when compared to those of other companies.

Formal Eligibility Criteria

How should a company go about selecting the specific positions for bonus eligibility? Some companies develop definite eligibility criteria and let the chips fall where they may. These criteria usually involve four types of cutoffs.

1. *Salary cutoff:* anyone with a base salary of $20,000 or more per year is included.
2. *Salary grade cutoff:* anyone assigned to compensation grade 18 or above is included.
3. *Organizational cutoff:* anyone in the top two levels directly below the president is included.
4. *Combination cutoffs:* anyone in the top two levels of the organization who is also in compensation grade 16 or above is included.

Cutoff 4 is the best approach, because types 1 to 3, when taken individually, contain problems. Salary cutoffs discriminate in favor of disciplines with a high market worth and often result in some lower-paid executives with important responsibilities being crowded off the list. Salary cutoffs also interrupt the smooth flow of salary payments. For example, there seemed to be no good reason why one company had 200 executives at $24,999 per year until it was learned that the company's bonus cutoff was $25,000 per year.

Salary grade cutoffs present fewer problems than salary cutoffs but again are unduly influenced by the market worth considerations that went into the compensation structure design.

Organizational level cutoffs are too easily subject to political tampering and as a result often lead to the inclusion of individuals with relatively minor responsibilities and the exclusion of individuals with truly major responsibilties.

Formal eligibility criteria should be established only after the fact and should be used to rationalize the eligibility selections that have already been made. This approach involves a critical examination of each executive position, from the top down. It will be readily apparent that some positions *must* be included. It will be just as apparent that other positions should not be included. And there will be a group of borderline positions. At this point, tentative decisions should be made on each borderline position. Then the designer should attempt to formulate eligibility criteria which include all the selections that have been made and exclude all other personnel in the company. Probably no set of simple yet meaningful criteria can be designed to do the job perfectly, and as a result some problem cases will crop up—a few eligibles who would be knocked off the list by the formal criteria and a few noneligibles who would be added to the list. Just as probably, these problem cases will all have been included in the original group of borderline eligibles. The company may well decide to accept these minor revisions dictated by the formal eligibility criteria.

Used in this manner, such criteria impose a sort of discipline on the company and facilitate an optimum degree of internal equity.

Once these criteria have been drawn, deviations should *never* be permitted without a total redesign of the criteria themselves. Since the criteria break what was essentially a continuum of responsibilities and are therefore somewhat arbitrary, even one deviation can lead to the demise of the whole system.

To illustrate, a company decided to employ a status type of badge system. Supervisors were given red badges, and nonsupervisory exempt personnel were given candy-striped badges. The system was arbitrary, but as long as everyone understood how it worked there were no problems. One day a high-level engineering specialist who was not a supervisor turned up at the personnel director's office. "This system is ridiculous," he complained. "Here I am in a very important job earning three times what those foremen in the factory earn, and they look down their noses at me because they have a red badge and I have a candy-striped one. I can't get my job done without a red badge!"

The personnel director made what turned out to be a fatal decision: He agreed to give the engineer a red badge. Of course, once he received his new badge, the engineer ran as fast as he could to his work group and began to flaunt his new status symbol. Naturally, engineers made the trip to the personnel office in a steady stream. "We understood the system before," they said, "but if Joe is going to have a red badge, we have to have one also." They too received red badges and were then followed by individuals in other disciplines who heard what good results could be obtained from a visit to the personnel office.

Pretty soon, there were so many red badges around that the candy-striped badges became status symbols in their own right.

Eventually, the company had to eliminate the whole program and substitute a uniform badge for all exempt personnel, thereby losing the status advantages of the previous system. By the same token, a company which deviates from its arbitrary rules governing bonus eligibility is going to be faced with the same problem.

Informing an Executive of His Eligibility

Once the eligibility rules have been established, people who are eligible should be informed. In effect, they should be told that they will receive an award each year or be given the reasons for not receiving one. Informing the individual of his eligibility has two advantages. First, it motivates him to go after the prize. In short, it puts the carrot in front of the horse rather than behind it. Second, it gives him considerable status in the eyes of his associates. Status is just another word for recognition, and recognition is a motivator.

Of course, such an approach may create some dissatisfaction among those who didn't make the eligibility list. But at least it clears up a question in many executives' minds: "Was I considered for an award and found lacking, or was I not considered at all?"

Special Awards

As noted earlier, the company should also provide special, one-shot awards to personnel not regularly eligible to participate. On rare occasions, an individual in a lower-level position makes an unexpected contribution which *does* have a very significant impact on the company's success. Examples of these types of contributions are an engineer who achieves a vital technological breakthrough and a purchasing agent who discovers a way to save the company a million dollars.

By definition, such contributions are not going to occur very often, and it is highly unlikely that the same individual will turn in performance of this magnitude two years in a row. The number of special awards is therefore going to be small—probably no more than 15 percent of the regular awards in any one year.

The advantage of special awards is that they help to blur, even if only a little, the arbitrary line of demarcation between regular eligibility and noneligibility. People who are not eligible understand that all hope is not lost and that magnificent performance will not go unrewarded.

There is a danger in special awards, however, and that is that the tail may wag the dog. At one huge company, the typical practice was to give 1,800 special awards each year, yet the regular eligibility list totaled only 1,000. When asked what percentage received special awards in two successive years, the personnel executive replied, "Oh, about 95 percent." Obviously, there was no longer anything special about that company's special awards.

Special awards, like regular awards, must be meaningful if they are truly to motivate. At the same company, the average special award was 3 percent of salary. When asked if awards of this level really motivated anybody, the personnel executive replied, "They're certainly not motivational, but we'd get one hell of a lot of demotivation if we cut them out!" His point illustrates the fact that companies can, if they are not careful, fall into a compensation trap from which it is very difficult to get free.

Award Levels

Awards should be both meaningful in size and at least competitive with the practices of other companies. They should also vary according to the position level. Exhibit 2, shown earlier, indicates that the *average* bonus award as a percentage of salary in a diversified group of manufacturers ranges from 20 percent at the $20,000 base salary level to 80 percent at the $250,000 base salary level. There are two reasons to support the validity of this trend, one more pragmatic than the other.

First, the higher the position, the more visible the accomplishments or failures of the incumbent. And the more conspicuous the incumbent, the more risk he takes, for mediocrity of performance at high levels will not be tolerated for long. As noted earlier, a high degree of risk must carry a high degree of reward.

Second, the higher the position, the higher the incumbent's base salary. And the higher the base salary, the higher the marginal income tax rate for additional ordinary income. Therefore, unless those in higher positions receive a greater percentage of pretax reward, their after-tax yield as a percentage of their after-tax salary will be less than that of others in lower-level positions.

These bonus ranges of 20 to 80 percent are, as noted, merely averages. Since any average is made up of a series of numbers, some higher and some lower, it follows that maximum bonus opportunities must be even greater than 20 to 80 percent. A maximum guideline of 130 percent of the average was used earlier in designing the integrated total compensation structure; applying this guideline to the 20 to 80 percent average produces potential maximum awards in the range of 56 to 134 percent of base salary ($20,000 base + 20 percent average bonus = $24,000 × 130 percent = $31,200 or 156 percent of base; $250,000 base + 80 percent average bonus = $450,000 × 130 percent = $585,000 or 234 percent of base).

In a way, these figures represent minimum maximums. If a company wants to pay its outstanding performers more than they could receive as outstanding performers at other companies, then it would do well to consider ever higher maximums. General Motors, for example, pays bonuses as high as 300 percent of base salary, and its late great president Alfred Sloan, for one, felt that the company's magnificent bonus opportunities were a critical factor in making it the company that it is.

Using the Integrated Compensation Ranges

We have been discussing bonus awards as percentages of base salary in order to illustrate certain trends, but such awards should really be administered in dollar terms within the integrated compensation structure to avoid possible pyramiding of compensation and the creation of other inequities.

Consider these two instances. First, we have an executive whose performance is outstanding but whose salary of $32,000 is 20 percent below the going rate. Our hypothetical company, employing the bonus curve shown in Exhibit 2, has adopted a policy calling for a 30 percent bonus for average performance and a 70 percent bonus for outstanding performance. Thus the executive receives a bonus of $22,400 (70 percent of $32,000) and total compensation of $54,400. The problem in this case is that the 70 percent competitive bonus for outstanding performance was predicated on a salary equal to the going rate of $40,000; by rights, the executive should therefore have received total compensation of $68,000, which at his current salary rate of $32,000, would have required a 113 percent bonus.

Second, we have another executive in the same type of job as the first executive. His salary of $48,000 is 20 percent above the competitive rate but his performance is only average. Under the company's policy, he will receive a 30 percent bonus, giving him total compensation of $62,400. By rights, his bonus should have been predicated on the going rate and not on his actual salary. Applying a 30 percent bonus to a $40,000 salary produces total compensation of $52,000. Thus the bonus in this case should have been only $4,000.

By using a percentage-of-base-salary approach to bonus determination, therefore, a company does very little to correct the inequities it currently has in its salary payments. And even when the compensation gap principle is used in salary determination, as discussed in Chapter 4, there are still going to be some salary inequities somewhere.

Thus award levels should be established not as a percentage of salary but as the dollar distance between the individual's current base salary and the targeted position in the total compensation range that has been established for his performance level. Such an approach corrects rather than perpetuates compensation inequities.

Of course, one concomitant of this approach is that the dollar amount of bonus paid to an individual whose salary is below his targeted range point will decrease as his salary approaches its correct level, unless he is simultaneously improving his performance. This pattern is considered to be demotivating by some executives. But again it comes down to a matter of choice. It seems far better to pay a man what he is worth when he is worth it than to keep him underpaid and create the illusion of steady growth. An executive searcher will tell it like it is the next time the phone rings—and there goes the illusion.

Establishing the Goals

The implicit goals of most incentive plans can be found by examining the funding formulas the companies employ. These in turn are typically centered around only one objective, such as return on invested capital, return on assets, return on capital employed, earnings per share, or dividend payments. And whatever the single objective chosen, it is almost always based on a single year's results.

Thus we have an overly simplistic approach to incentive compensation. There is not one but a number of important goals in any business. And, with increasingly complex technology stretching out product lead times, maximizing results in any single year can sow the seeds of trouble for future years.

On the other hand, we have to consider the shareholder reaction. Any complicated formula is unlikely to be easily understood, thereby leading many shareholders to feel that the company is playing some trick which will hurt them.

Of course, there is nothing to prevent a company from using a single-objective, single-year funding formula for shareholder approval and ultimate control purposes and then distributing the funds in a manner which reflects progress against multiple goals, stretching over more than one year if necessary. Because companies are trapped in the inertia created by the shareholder-approved funding formula, they do not do this—but they should.

The Internal Funding Formula

The first step in developing an internal funding formula is the establishment of corporate and, where the company is decentralized, divisional goals. Like those formulated for individual executives, there can be several, comprising both qualitative and quantitative elements. Moreover, if the company is involved in high-technology products, with attendant swings in year-to-year performance owing to long product development lead times, these goals can be established for longer than a one-year period (two years, three years, and so on) and then subdivided into annual installments for purposes of making incentive progress payments.

Thus a company can have an internal funding formula based on goals for sales, profits, research and development, personnel development, and any other combination of objectives which are meaningful to that particular business at that particular time.

Like the system described earlier for individual performance appraisal, these sets of goals are weighted to reflect their relative importance. And the same 50- to 150-point rating scheme (or whatever other scheme the company wishes) is utilized, with enough stretch built into each goal that its attainment clearly connotes outstanding performance. Subsidiary point schedules for various levels of less-than-outstanding performance can also be established in advance for the quantitative goals, such as sales and profits.

In a decentralized company, a set of goals can be established for each division, but there might also be a set of overall internal corporate goals based on a consolidation of the divisions' goals. (More will be said later about the purpose of using both corporate and divisional goals in a decentralized company.)

At the end of the year, the previously weighted goals (or a portion thereof if the goals cover more than one year) are rated using the subsidiary point schedules and, in the case of the qualitative goals, management judgment. As in the procedure described earlier, weightings can be multiplied by ratings and an overall point score obtained for the unit being appraised. This overall point score becomes the basis for an internal funding formula, which in turn generates the monies needed for individual awards.

The funds needed for a given unit in a given year under given performance conditions are built up using each grade of the integrated total compensation structure. For average unit performance (point rating of 100), the funds required for each compensation grade would equal the difference between the total compensation control point and the base salary control point multiplied by the number of eligible executives assigned to that compensation grade. The sums for each compensation grade would be totaled and the resulting figure increased by a specified percentage to provide for special awards for those not regularly eligible to participate in the plan (most companies allow 10 to 15 percent of the total fund to be diverted for special awards).

For outstanding unit performance (point rating of 150), the funds for each compensation grade should equal the difference between the total compensation maximum and the base salary control point multiplied by the number of eligible executives assigned to that grade. The sums for each compensation grade are then totaled, but in this case no provision for special awards is made. The reason is that in an outstanding year, not every regular eligible will be considered outstanding. Therefore, ample funds should be left over to fund the special award segment of the plan.

We now have the funds required for average performance (point rating of 100) and for outstanding performance (point rating of 150). All that remains is to establish the funding at each performance point between 50 and 150 by constructing a curve which starts at zero dollars for 50 performance points and reaches the required funding for average performance at 100 points and for outstanding performance at 150 points. The slope of this curve should contain an acceleration factor similar to the one established for the subsidiary point schedules covering the quantitative objectives. An example of this type of acceleration was shown earlier. (The curve will probably progress naturally at a steeper rate from 100 to 150 points than from 50 to 100 points. Nevertheless, the company may want more acceleration, depending on what is used in the subsidiary point schedules for the quantitative objectives.)

Two points should be observed in connection with the development of the internal funding formulas. First, funds are being created even when the overall unit's performance is less than average (between 50 and 100 performance points). Such an approach seems to contradict the principle that awards should never be paid for less than average performance. However, even in the year of poorest overall performance, there are likely to be a few individuals whose performance is average or better. Additionally, there are going to be some noneligible personnel who have earned a special award. Thus a modest fund must be created even when the unit's overall performance is below average. (Keeping the funds truly "modest" is another reason for putting an acceleration factor on the fund-generation curve. In that way, the amount of funds remains miniscule until, say, the 85 to 90 performance point level is reached.)

The second point to be noted is that the funding requirements are predicated not on the eligibles' actual salaries but on base salary control points. It is important to follow this procedure if the company wishes to avoid funding distortions and the possible creation of excessive funds.

The External Funding Formula

We now turn to the external funding formula—the one that may be submitted for the shareholders' approval.

The external funding formula may be conceived of as a sort of circuit breaker. And like its electrical counterpart, it cuts in when things go wrong. Such an approach is vitally necessary when internal formulas are being utilized, because a company may be too lax in setting its internal goals and too lenient in rating these goals—especially the qualitative ones.

An external funding formula protects the shareholders from problems of this type and insures that the total amount of funds provided for incentive awards is reasonable and in line with the company's ability to pay.

As mentioned earlier, the typical external funding formula is based on (1) return on invested capital, (2) return on capital employed (invested capital plus long-term debt), or (3) return on assets—listed in the order of their popularity.

Although there are no hard or fast rules for selecting the most desirable of these measures for any one company, return on invested capital has been given the edge probably because most analysts feel that it represents the ultimate reason why the company is in business. Furthermore, in this day of asset management, the use of debt for leverage purposes is being given great play, and obviously an approach using return on capital employed or return on assets would be unrewarding from a leverage standpoint.

Pretax Versus After-Tax Profits

The numerator used in the return-on-invested-capital equation is pretax profits in some companies and after-tax profits in others. The trend, however, is definitely to the use of pretax profits because federal income tax rates are outside the control of the company's executives. There is a hard-core minority, nevertheless, that advocates the after-tax profits approach because tax rates are not a variable unto themselves but spill over into other areas of the business and hence affect vital decisions. Certainly, after-tax profits is the preferred measure in industries such as banking, where, by varying the mixture of tax-exempt bonds, the company can materially affect its effective tax rate. Except in such special circumstances, however, the majority opinion is preferable.

Before the company's profits are plugged into the numerator of the return equation, one or more of three different adjustments usually occur. First, reserves have been built up during the year for anticipated bonus awards, and these have already been deducted. Hence they must be added back. (It is noteworthy here that companies which use after-tax profits usually add back the full amount of the bonus reserve—a pretax figure—rather than adding back only the after-tax equivalent of this figure.)

The second adjustment is restricted to formulas using return on capital employed or return on assets as the basis of performance, and it involves adding back the interest payments on long-term debt. These interest payments, like the bonus reserves, have already been deducted from the profit figure. Were such an approach not adopted, the company would be penalized twice for borrowing: once when the principal sum borrowed was added to the denominator and once again when the interest payments caused the profits to decline. Some companies, however, have failed to realize this fact and have unnecessarily diminished the amount of their bonus funds. Plans using return on invested capital do not require adding back the interest on long-term debt because only one penalty is involved—in the numerator.

The third adjustment calls for the addition to or the subtraction from profits of extraordinary charges or credits which have little to do with the performance of the executive group. The one-time capital gain resulting from the sale of an entire division is an example of the extraordinary items that necessitate a profit adjustment.

The Deductible

The great majority of bonus formulas use what is termed a "deductible" and do not generate funds until the return reaches a certain level. Thus a typical formula might read: "10 percent of profits before provision for federal income taxes [adjusted as previously described] after first deducting from such profits an amount equal to 16 percent of invested capital as of the beginning of the year."

Other companies employ so-called sideline limitations either alone or in conjunction with a deductible. Thus, notwithstanding the formula, "funds may never exceed 25 percent of dividends declared"; or "no funds will be generated unless earnings per share are at least $1."

The use of a modified sideline limitation approach, which is described shortly, is better than the use of a deductible. The latter creates distortions in fund generation and makes it difficult to provide the proper amount of funds at various performance levels.

In the usual formula employing a deductible, there is little room between the deductible percentage and the percentage that represents average competitor performance. To achieve proper funding for average performance therefore requires that the company use a high multiplier for fund creation purposes—for example, 25 percent of profits in excess of the deductible. This solves the problem at the point of average corporate performance but creates two other problems in its wake. First, the multiplier is so high that if corporate performance turns out to be above average to outstanding, far too many dollars are generated. This factor and the visibly high multiplier itself combine to create potential problems with the company's shareholders.

The company can of course use a lower multiplier which produces the correct amount of funds at the level of outstanding performance, but then in years of average performance the company goes hungry insofar as proper bonuses are concerned.

An alternative solution that some companies have adopted involves the use of a high multiplier between the deductible and the point of average corporate performance

147

and a low multiplier above this point. A typical formula might read: "25 percent of profits before income taxes which are in excess of an amount equal to 16 percent of invested capital but are less than an amount equal to 24 percent of invested capital; plus 10 percent of all profits which are in excess of an amount equal to 24 percent of invested capital."

This solution involves a decelerating bonus formula, which, motivationally speaking, is completely wrong. As noted earlier, if the performance is already high, it is harder to obtain the next higher increment of performance.

In fact, unless the deductible formula contains an acceleration feature, it will automatically be decelerating—even when the multiplier is nominally constant. To illustrate, assume that a company had invested capital of $833 million and employed a formula which generated 3 percent of all profits in excess of the amount equal to 12 percent of invested capital. The deductible is therefore $100 million. If the company's profits were $110 million, the bonus fund would accordingly be $300,000 ($110 million − $100 million deductible = $10 million excess profits × 3 percent = $300,000). By increasing the company's profits in successive 10 percent intervals, here is what happens to the fund generation.

Profits (Millions)	Percent Increase over Previous Number	Fund Generation (Thousands)	Percent Increase over Previous Number
$110	—	$ 300	—
121	10	630	110
133	10	990	57
147	10	1,395	41

The use of a deductible caused a built-in disincentive effect in this company's plan. For each percentage increase in performance, the executives in this company received a smaller percentage increase in their bonus funds.

The Preferred Sideline Approach

The purpose of a deductible is primarily symbolic. It assures the shareholders that they are being put ahead of the executives. This purpose can be more effectively served by a formula utilizing the deductible's rationale—but employing a sideline limitation. For example, the formula just cited could be modified to read: "No funds will be created unless profits are equal to 12 percent of invested capital. Thereafter, the fund shall consist of the lower of (1) all profits in excess of an amount equal to 12 percent of invested capital or (2) 3 percent of total profits."

This approach continues to emphasize the primacy of the shareholders. Once profits reach the sideline limitation, however, there is no longer any deductible to create all the problems just discussed. A smooth buildup of funds is assured, starting with the first dollar of profit. (The alternative of diverting all funds in excess of a 12 percent return, if that would produce a lower amount than the straight 3 percent application, is merely to insure that profits, after creation of bonus funds, do not dip below the minimum 12 percent return level.)

Of course, this modified formula would create more funds than the first formula because it eliminates the deductible. This is another advantage, because a company could then adopt a lower multiplier for generating funds without sacrificing its funding objectives. The lower the multiplier, the less visible the plan and the less resistance from company shareholders. Another attribute of plans based on pretax profits over those based on after-tax profits is that a lower multiplier can be used because the profit base is larger. Similarly, a higher deductible or sideline limitation will be employed. Both factors diminish the visibilty of the plan.

Gearing the Formula to Industry Performance

A viable external funding formula should be geared not to what the company thinks is average and outstanding performance but to what is in fact average and outstanding performance by industry standards. To illustrate, a company has decided to employ an external funding formula featuring pretax return on invested capital as the measure of performance and a sideline limitation for shareholder protection similar to what was just described. The first step in determining the correct multiplier and sideline percentages is to study the competitors' pretax returns on invested capital. The results of several years, rather than simply the previous year, are used to provide some stability to the results. Suppose that, after studying data from 15 companies, the firm concludes that a 16 percent pretax return on invested capital represents minimal performance; a 24 percent return represents average performance; and a 32 percent return represents outstanding performance. Suppose further that the company has $400 million of invested capital and requires $1 million of bonus funding at the average corporate performance level and $3 million when corporate performance is outstanding. The company could therefore adopt the following formula: "No funds will be created unless pretax return on invested capital is equal to 16 percent. Thereafter, the fund will equal the lesser of (1) all profits in excess of an amount equal to 16 percent of invested capital or (2) 1 percent of all profits which are less than an amount equal to 24 percent of invested capital plus 6 percent of all profits which are in excess of an amount equal to 24 percent of invested capital."

Let us simulate this formula for average and outstanding performance. At a 24 percent return (average performance) on $400 million of invested capital, the company's pretax profits are $96 million. Applying the 1 percent multiplier to this figure produces a fund of $960,000, which is very close to the $1 million needed. (Decimalization could be used in the multiplier to achieve the precise result desired—but rarely is.)

At a 32 percent return (outstanding performance) on $400 million of invested capital, the company's pretax profits are $128 million. The 1 percent multiplier has, of course, already been used on the first $96 million to produce $960,000 of funds. The $32 million of additional profit above $96 million is then used to create the remaining funds. The 6 percent multiplier is applied to it, with the result that $1.92 million of additional funds are generated. Added to the $960,000 generated initially, a total of $2.88 million is produced for bonus purposes, and this amount is passably close to the $3 million originally required to reward outstanding performance.

Note that this formula contains the right sort of acceleration. It can demonstrate tangibly to the company's executives that there is a willingness to pay truly meaningful awards for above average to outstanding performance.

The formula resulting from this approach should be checked against the formulas of the company's competitors to see that it is reasonable. Such a check is of course hard to make because other companies' formulas contain a variety of differing elements. Some may be on a pretax basis; some on an after-tax basis; some with deductibles; some without deductibles; and so on. An approach that can be used to circumvent these problems, however, is to take the other companies' formulas and apply them to one's own profit and loss statement and balance sheet items to see what funds would be generated were such formulas in use at one's own company. The figures derived should be compared both singly and in the form of an average to the funds that would have resulted had the company's proposed formula been in effect during the same years as those of the other companies.

If the differences observed are minor, the company can be assured that its proposed formula is reasonable in light of the practices of other companies and that it has created an eligible group of proper size. If, on the other hand, the differences are major, something is probably wrong, and the first place to look is in the size of the proposed eligible group. Since the company started with industry average award levels, the problem could not be there. If, however, the company created too large or too small an eligible group, the funds it said it needed at various levels of corporate performance would differ materially from the funds created at those same levels by applying the other companies' formulas to its own profit and loss statement and balance sheet. Therefore, this cross-checking procedure becomes valuable as an additional tool in verifying the correctness of a company's decisions concerning bonus eligibility.

Extra Formula Limitations

Is the formula as developed here sufficient to protect shareholder interests, or should additional sideline limitations be added? Some companies use multiple devices to protect their shareholders. A good sideline limitation of the type just discussed is sufficient. It is important to be wary of using the common form of sideline limitation which requires that the fund not exceed a certain percentage of the dividends declared. Such a limitation may provide excellent "window dressing," but in the long run it may be injurious to the shareholder's interests because it might lead to a decision to increase dividends as a means of removing the effect of the limitation. Ostensibly, this would be great for the shareholders; but perhaps the money might have been put to better use by being reinvested in the business. In any event, sideline limitations should protect the shareholders, not create conflicts of interest within the company.

Dual Objectives in the External Funding Formula

An alternative approach to the subject of external funding formulas should be mentioned briefly. It calls for two measures of performance rather than only one. For instance, a company could use both return on invested capital and rate of growth in return on invested capital to design a bonus formula. The measures could be mixed in varying proportions, such that a high rate of growth in return on invested capital could partially offset a less than desirable return on invested capital compared to industry standards. Similarly, extra credit could be given to the company that does well in both areas.

153

These two factors, taken together, account for more of the variance in the market price of a company's stock than either factor does alone. The company's shareholders should therefore find such a plan appealing. And so should the company's executives because more funds for bonuses are available when the company's performance, although less than the industry average, is improving at a good rate.

Disposing of Surplus Bonus Funds

Another factor to consider in bonus formula design is the disposition of surplus funds that are not needed for bonuses in the current year. Such surpluses may accumulate because there aren't enough outstanding executives in an outstanding year to soak up the entire bonus fund. Some companies restore such surpluses to net income and others retain them for use in future years.

Without viable internal fund generation formulas, surpluses should be restored to net income; if they are carried over to future years, management may yield to the temptation of using them as a means of equalizing executive bonuses from one year to the next, thereby reducing the differential between periods of excellent and poor corporate performance. On the other hand, carrying over surplus bonuses can be of assistance in unusual situations—for example, when one or two divisions in a company have such a disastrous year that they cancel out the funds generated by all—even the satisfactory—divisions.

With good internal fund-generating formulas which help to insure that bonus funds are used in a maximally motivating manner, there would appear to be no problem with the retention of surplus bonus funds from year to year.

Revising the Formula

Formulas, like tires, do not last forever. Accordingly, a company's formula should undergo periodic inspection to see whether it needs retreading or replacement.

Contrary to some executives' impressions, the company should not experience difficulty in finding the funds for awards to new eligibles—provided that the company's growth makes the addition of new eligibles justified. If the formula is predicated on, say, return on investment, a doubling of invested capital and the maintenance of the same percentage return on that invested capital will yield double the funds. Since a doubling in company size is unlikely to warrant a doubling in the number of eligibles, the company may indeed be a little better off.

Another problem that may arise is that the industry may change its standards of performance. Suppose, for example, the average return on invested capital for an entire industry drops significantly over a period of years, owing perhaps to increased government regulation or a change in IRS rules concerning deductibility of business expenses or depreciation. In this event, the company will undoubtedly have trouble meeting the standards of previous years, and its bonus fund will be materially reduced. Yet, judged by the new industry standards, the company may be doing an excellent job.

The reverse can occur also. With rising industry standards of performance, the company's bonus plan is likely to become overfunded. Although this problem is not too hard to take, it should nevertheless be corrected before too much time has passed.

In cases such as these, the company may have to redesign its bonus formula. The procedure is identical to the

155

one followed for the original formula. And, of course, the new formula should receive all the necessary tests, including a test on past company results, to insure that it is reasonable, produces meaningful award funds, and is well within the company's ability to pay.

Handling Bonus Erosion

The one bonus formula problem that cannot—and should not—be corrected through a change in the formula is lack of funds caused by an unjustified and significant increase in the number of eligibles. All bonus plans erode over time. Little by little, more and more people become eligible, and thus the number of special awards rises. At first, the company handles this erosion by cutting down on the size of each bonus.

Eventually, this approach becomes counterproductive when the original group of eligibles starts complaining. It is at this time that management looks wistfully at its formula and thinks, "Just one little percentage point more on that multiplier would take care of all our problems." This is not an effective or even an ethical solution, because one of the reasons the formula was designed around industry performance standards was to control this very problem. Even today, a few companies use a funding formula which gives management a sort of "bonus bounty"—$5,000 for each regular eligible. Needless to say, the growth in the number of eligibles is about the only growth these companies seem to be achieving.

The obvious, albeit painful, remedy for bonus erosion is to reduce the number of eligibles until sufficient funds are available to provide meaningful awards.

Allocating the Bonus Fund

Once the bonus formula has been created and is in operation, management has to decide how the overall funds produced are to be allocated among the major divisions and departments. The company can, of course, eliminate this step entirely and go directly to the determination of individual awards, but such an approach is ill-advised and akin to juggling 200 balls at once.

There seem to be as many different allocation procedures as there are companies. Some companies simply make a pro rata distribution to their divisions and departments. This approach, however, does not stimulate one division or department to turn in an outstanding performance when the corporation as a whole has a mediocre year.

Another and better approach is to determine the funds that would be payable to each unit for average and outstanding unit performance, based on the number of eligibles in the unit and their compensation grade assignments. Next, the overall company fund, minus awards for the chairman and president and special awards, is converted into a "normal award pattern" by calculating its relationship to the distance between aggregate awards payable for average performance and aggregate awards payable for outstanding performance. Thus, assume the funds required to give all remaining eligibles an award for average performance were $1 million and the funds required to give all remaining eligibles an award for outstanding performance were $3 million, and the overall fund itself (after the adjustments described) were $2.5 million. The normal award pattern for each unit of the company would then be the unit's aggregate awards for average performance plus 75 percent of the difference between the unit's aggregate awards for average performance and for outstanding performance.

If each unit were adjudged the performance equal of every other unit, then each would receive its normal award pattern as previously established. Probably, however, some units will have turned in better performance than others, and adjustments in normal award patterns will therefore have to be made. In most companies that employ this procedure, the adjustments are made by the president on a purely judgmental basis. Of course, an increase in one unit's normal award pattern must necessarily result in a decrease in some other unit's pattern.

A far better approach and one which is more motivational is to establish separate internal divisional funding formulas, as described here. In this manner, the division executives can see in advance what rewards are likely to result from their actions. Since they will probably perceive that they are more in control of these rewards, they will tend to work harder to achieve them.

Corporate Versus Individual Unit Incentives

Although organizations undergo decentralization as a means of fostering a more entrepreneurial attitude on the part of divisional executives, in the final analysis these individuals remain part of the corporation as a whole. And thus to some extent they must share in the company's failures and successes in other divisions.

Therefore, divisional executives should look partly to their own internal funding formulas and partly to the company's overall internal funding formula for their total awards. This allocation between corporate and divisional performance can be made very simply. Suppose, for example, that the basic allocation between corporate and divisional performance is set at 20 percent for corporate performance and 80 percent for divisional performance. Suppose further that the aggregate awards payable to all divisional eligibles for outstanding performance is $500,000. The division's own internal funding formula is then established to generate $400,000 for outstanding performance. The remaining $100,000 is placed in the overall company internal funding formula and is generated when the company as a whole achieves its outstanding performance objectives.

With this type of approach, the division receives maximum funds only when both it and the company as a whole perform outstandingly. On the other hand, the division's funds are reduced when it performs in an outstanding manner but the company doesn't. Divisional funds can also be increased—beyond what they would have been had this procedure not been adopted—when the company as a whole outperforms the division.

Some company presidents who initially welcomed decentralization have come to regret their decision, for as Antony Jay observed in *Management and Machiavelli: An Inquiry into the Politics of Corporate Life*, "When the barons are strong, the king is weak." [1]

By requiring that divisional executives look to the success of the company as a whole for part of their rewards, the company's top management stands to gain some additional cooperation and therefore perhaps some of that elusive quality known as synergy.

[1] New York: Holt, Rinehart and Winston, 1968.

Correcting for Compensation Pyramiding

It will be recalled that an above average executive receives performance recognition by being granted an above average salary, an above average bonus, or a combination of both. It will also be recalled that the preferred method of bonus funding involves the use of base salary control points rather than actual base salaries of the eligible group. This approach presents a problem when the eligibles' actual aggregate salaries are greater than their actual aggregate base salary control points, because an identical amount of money has already been built into the bonus formula. Without correction, the executives would be paid more than once for the same performance. To correct this, the amount by which the eligibles' actual salaries exceed their aggregate base salary control points should simply be deducted from the funds produced by the organizational unit's own funding formula.

Correcting for Insufficient Compensation

Of course, the reverse could happen, and insufficient bonus funds could be provided to "top up the tank" when the eligibles' actual salaries are less than their aggregate base salary control points. It is tempting in this case to add additional funds to those produced by the formula, because it takes pressure off the company to bring its executives' salaries up to competitive levels—but this temptation must be resisted. Since salary levels largely govern the magnitude of many fringe benefits, such as pension and profit-sharing plans, life insurance coverage, and so on, the problem can be further exacerbated.

Determining Individual Awards

When overall bonus funds have been created and chunks of these funds have been allocated to various units of the company, the next step in the award process is to determine the amount of each eligible's award and to make special awards to deserving noneligibles.

Some companies pay awards on a group basis. Each eligible receives a proportionate share based on the relationship between his salary and the salaries of all other eligibles. This approach may encourage teamwork, but it may also encourage indolence as executives whose performance might otherwise be outstanding adjust their contributions to the lowest common denominator.

Moreover, the group award approach tends to magnify inequities in the company's current salary payments. For example, if one executive is making $20,000 but should be making $30,000, and another executive is making $30,000 but should be making $20,000, and both receive a 50 percent group award, the result widens the inequity between these executives from an initial figure of $10,000 to an ultimate figure of $15,000.

Other companies avoid the group award approach entirely and base awards solely on individual performance. Implicit in their choice is the assumption that if they motivate the individual, the teamwork will take care of itself. In any event, they will see to it that managerial backbiting doesn't become too pronounced.

Many of these same companies are deceiving themselves, however, when they say that they are truly rewarding individual performance. Two examples illustrate this fact.

A few years ago, a comprehensive survey of 12 companies' executive bonus plans was conducted. After asking how many people were eligible for bonus consideration, the following routine question was asked: "How many eligibles actually receive a bonus in a typical year?" Of the 12 companies asked, 9 had 90 percent or more of bonus eligibles; one had 86 percent; one had 75 percent; and one had 50 percent. It can be readily seen that these companies give most of their executives a bonus every year. Yet, in answer to an earlier question, every one of these companies stated that bonuses were awarded for outstanding performance only!

Because these results were puzzling, the companies were further asked: "If you give bonuses only for outstanding performance, how is it that such a high percentage of your eligible executives qualify each year?" After first appearing surprised at being asked such a question, most of the respondents gave a rather patronizing answer. "Well, it should be perfectly obvious," they said. "Our executives would never have made it to the positions they occupy if they weren't outstanding."

This answer demonstrates a subtle but fundamental flaw in the manner in which many companies view their top management personnel. Certainly, these executives are outstanding—certainly, "the cream rises to the top"; but there are many grades of cream, and some are better than others. The only proper basis of performance assessment for an executive, therefore, is to compare him to his peers both in his own company and in others. On this basis, it is obvious that not every executive is outstanding. In fact, there is no reason to believe that executive performance, like the performance of other groups, is not distributed in a purely Gaussian manner. Accordingly, somewhere in the United States there have to be as many incompetent executives as there are outstanding ones.

What about the two companies in the survey with relatively reasonable percentages of eligibles receiving awards? Surely, here we have two examples of companies with enlightened management. Unfortunately, however, both companies had eligible lists numbering several thousand, and the data analysis indicated that the lower award frequency was coming out of the hides of the lowest-paid eligibles. In effect, better than 90 percent of the upper-level executives were receiving bonuses, but only around 25 percent of the lower-level executives were. Since the latter far outnumbered the former, the overall result made the company look good.

In another case, a company's bonus data showed what apparently was some evidence of performance discrimination. There was no one percentage of bonus for every executive—even when the effects of lower and higher salaries were factored out. The same applied to data from the previous year's bonus. Bonuses, however, were considerably lower in the current year than in the previous year. An examination of the funding formula showed that total bonus funds in the current year were only 60 percent of those generated in the previous year. Just for the fun of it, a few further checks were made, and these showed that every executive's bonus in the current year was precisely 60 percent of the bonus he received in the previous year. Thus, having rated each executive's relative performance contribution several years back, this company assumed that each executive was continuing to make precisely the same relative contribution every year.

These two illustrations show how hard it is to reward performance in a truly discriminating manner. Top managers in many companies grasp at any available rationalization to avoid making gutty performance assessments. They use the vertical rating error; or they increase or decrease individual bonuses from year to year only as the total amount of funds increases or decreases. Or they convince themselves that to withhold a bonus from an individual who has had one for several years running will either ruin his motivation or compromise his standard of living. In truly desperate cases, both reasons are advanced.

There is no simple answer to this problem. Only the implementation of a rational and valid performance appraisal system, such as the one described earlier, and a good dose of management guts will bring a solution.

One thing that a company should not do is allow the normal-award concept of allocation discussed earlier to spill over into the establishment of award ranges. For example, suppose a company has an award range of 30 to 60 percent of salary for a given class of executives. If the funds allocated to a given unit are not enough to produce a good award for each executive in this bracket (say, 45 percent of salary), then the entire range of awards might be reduced proportionately. Thus, if the funds allocated are only enough to produce an average award of 30 percent of salary —a $33\frac{1}{3}$ percent reduction—the entire award range might be reduced by $33\frac{1}{3}$ percent and a new award range of 20 to 40 percent substituted.

A number of companies utilize this process, but it is wrong, because it assumes that every eligible will receive an award no matter how poorly the company performs.

In one division of a company, every eligible executive received an award one year. The smallest award was 3 percent of salary and the largest was 5 percent. The division manager was asked: "Why were your awards so small?" He replied, "Because we had a bad year in our division and the president gave us a tiny allocation."

He was asked another question: "Do you think that the difference between 3 percent of salary and 5 percent of salary adequately reflects the difference between your worst-performing and your best-performing executive?" "Oh, of course not," he said, "but you see, the funds were so small—what could I do?" It was then suggested, "Perhaps you could have given nothing to 15 out of your 20 eligible executives and used your entire allocation to grant significant rewards to just a few really outstanding individuals." "That's an interesting thought," he said, "but we *always* give everyone an award each year, so of course that idea simply wouldn't work."

Ranking the Eligibles

One approach that can be of assistance in determining individual awards is to rank all eligibles in descending order of their relative performance contributions. The word "relative" is key, for an individual who accomplishes less on an absolute basis than another but more in terms of what he *could have accomplished* would receive the higher ranking.

Having established the performance ranking, the executive making the award decisions starts from the top and works down. The individual ranked first receives an amount of bonus which when added to his salary will give him total compensation appropriate to his rating. (No reductions are ever made in bonus opportunities to reflect the size of the unit's allocation.) The same procedure is then followed for the second-ranked individual, the third, and so on until there are no funds left.

It is very likely that some individuals at the bottom of

the list will receive no awards. And the smaller the amount of funds available for awards, the larger this group will be. Before making his final decision, however, the reviewer should consider whether there are one or two marginal cases just below the award cutoff line who should perhaps receive the minimum award amount. If he decides in the affirmative, the reviewer will have to readjust the dollars assigned to various individuals above the cutoff to provide the necessary funds for these last one or two awards.

Therein lies the value of this procedure, for the executive making the award decisions is vividly reminded at every turn that the dollars required to give lower-ranked individuals any award at all in a year of less than fully outstanding unit performance will have to come out of the pockets of those whose performance contributions are considered greater. Recognizing this truth, the executives may be impelled to let the chips fall where they may, thereby increasing the motivational value of the company's bonus plan through the significant recognition that is implied in granting some executives maximum awards and others no awards at all.

Combination Group and Individual Awards

Some companies follow the policy of employing a combination of group and individual incentive awards in much the same manner that other companies weight divisional allocations with both the division's results and those of the corporation as a whole. In effect, the companies employing the combination approach seek to emphasize both teamwork and individual achievement and, in a way, obtain the best of both worlds.

Under this system, a given percentage of the overall fund (usually 20 to 40 percent) is distributed on a group basis. Every eligible executive receives this group distribution, which is usually prorated to salary. The remainder of the fund is then distributed on the basis of individual performance contributions.

If a company is going to employ a combination approach, the group award portion should really be prorated to award ranges and not to salary to avoid causing inequities. The range of awards, stated as a percentage of base salary, increases as the salary increases. Suppose, for example, that the highest range of awards, applicable to the president, was 30 to 90 percent of salary and the lowest range of awards was 10 to 30 percent of salary.

Suppose further that 25 percent of any funds generated was to be paid in the form of a group award. If the company has an outstanding year and a fund is generated sufficient to pay every eligible his maximum award, then the group award could—and should—consist of 25 percent of each eligible's award maximum. Thus the eligible with the highest award range would receive 22.5 percent of salary as a group award; and the eligibles with the lowest award range would receive 7.5 percent of salary.

If, on the other hand, the awards had been strictly prorated to base salary, every eligible would have received the same award percentage. As a result, the proportion of total award opportunity represented by the group award would unwittingly have been made significantly higher for the lowest-paid eligibles than for the highest-paid eligibles. Distributing group awards in proportion to the award ranges avoids these problems, although it does appear perhaps less democratic.

The proponents of the combination group-individual

award approach, besides emphasizing its value in motivating both teamwork and individual achievement, believe that it may eliminate the tendency to water down awards. Everyone gets at least the group award, so the theory goes, and therefore top managers will see to it that only the good performers get anything more. Presumably they will have the guts to make this approach stick, because they can take comfort in the fact that the mediocre performer did get something. Of course, some of the monies appropriated for group awards might have been better spent on the outstanding performers, but nevertheless, the combination approach may have some definite merit if it can achieve its designer's objectives.

The integrated compensation structure and the philosophy of closing compensation gaps can be used profitably in plans featuring both group and individual awards. Essentially, the proper amount of individual award is the difference between the executive's base salary plus his group award and the position in his total compensation range that is appropriate for his performance contributions. However, a large group award granted in a year of outstanding corporate performance can, when combined with base salary, push the average-performing executive's total compensation beyond his appropriate range position. In such a case, no further individual bonus would be indicated.

A further advantage of the combination approach is its use as a transition device for the company that is moving from a purely group distribution plan to one based solely on individual performance. Typically, this company cannot make the switch overnight because it lacks the precision performance assessment infrastructure needed to support individually determined bonuses. But the company can adopt a combination plan, starting with, say, 90 percent of the funds distributed on a group basis and 10 percent on an individual basis. With each passing year, the group percentage can be decreased and the individual performance percentage increased until one day the company has almost painlessly achieved its initial objective. On its way down, the company may of course find some combination of group and individual awards that is particularly beneficial, and, if so, there is no reason for it not to stop right there.

Minimum Awards

Technically an executive should receive the exact amount of bonus necessary to raise his total compensation to his appropriate range position, but that amount should not be granted unless it is meaningful. A number of alternative approaches can be used to achieve this objective. For example, awards can be restricted to payments of at least 10 percent of salary; or 10 percent of salary but not less than $3,000; or a minimum 10 percent of salary for the lowest level of eligibles, tapering up to 20 percent for the highest level. All these approaches are workable; the best one considers organization size, salary distribution of the eligible group, and the range of bonus opportunities.

Automatic Awards for the Chairman and President

Awards for the chairman and president are particularly difficult to determine because there is usually a built-in conflict of interest. Although most companies have a committee of the board of directors assigned to approve incentive compensation awards, this committee is pretty much at the mercy of the top executives when it comes to receiving the data on which to base its decisions. Then again, the chairman and president are board members. Thus, determining awards for them is both difficult and often embarrassing for the individuals involved.

One way of resolving this problem is to provide for automatic awards to the chairman and president—unless the board deliberately acts to override the formula amount. Ultimately, the performance of the two top men is measured by the company's overall performance. And, since the company's overall performance determines the bonus funds that will be provided, it makes sense to tie the awards for the chairman and president to the corporate internal funding formula. In effect, the overall point rating derived for this formula could also be assigned as the personal performance point rating of the chairman and president. (If the internal funding formula is too heavily weighted by subjective goals whose ratings are judgmentally assigned by the chairman or president, the external funding formula could be substituted to avoid another conflict of interest.) The awards for the chairman and the president would then be based on the relationship of the actual total funds generated to those that would have been generated at 100 and 150 overall corporate performance points.

To illustrate, assume that the overall corporate fund is $1 million at 100 points and $3 million at 150 points and that the chairman (who is earning a salary equal to the base salary control point of his range) is entitled to a bonus of $30,000 at 100 personal performance points and $100,000 at 150 personal performance points. If the overall fund is $3 million, the chairman will of course receive his maximum $100,000 award; in the same manner, he will receive his minimum award of $30,000 if the overall fund is $1 million. Suppose, however, that the fund is $2.5 million. Since this figure represents the minimum fund plus 75 percent of the difference between the overall minimum and maximum award funds, the chairman's award will then be $82,500—or his minimum award of $30,000 plus 75 percent of the difference between his minimum and maximum awards. The same process will then be followed for the president.

No awards would be paid to the chairman and president when overall corporate performance was below the 100 performance point level, since such performance would be below average, and no individual awards should be paid for below average performance. The small amount of funds generated between 50 and 100 corporate performance points should be reserved for more worthy performers.

Time of Payment and Award Media

Having established the amount of award that a given executive is to receive, the company must also decide on the time and method of payment. Payment can be made in full at the time the award is declared or it can be deferred. (Deferred payments are considered later.)

In essence, the choice of payment media involves cash or something other than cash. And the something other than cash almost always is company stock—at least where immediate payments are concerned. There are usually no great advantages or disadvantages to either approach. The tax consequences are the same in both instances; the individual must pay full ordinary income tax rates on the cash received or on the market value of the stock as of the date it is paid to him.

If company stock is used as the payment medium, the executive is of course free to convert his stock to cash at any time (unless unregistered shares are used, but this rarely occurs in immediate cash payments). If the award is entirely in company stock, the executive will probably cash at least part of it within a few months, inasmuch as the taxes on the entire award will come due shortly. For this reason, some companies prefer to give the executive a mixture of cash and company stock, such that the amount of cash paid is approximately equivalent to the amount of taxes on the entire award. With this approach, higher-paid executives receive a greater proportion of cash because of the influence of the progressive tax structure.

Since the underlying hope in using company stock for an immediate bonus payment is that the executive will retain as much of it as possible, other companies prefer to pay the entire award in stock, recognizing that, although most executives will cash some of it for tax purposes, others may be able to meet their tax payments with outside income and retain all the stock.

If treasury shares are used, the choice between all stock and part cash and part stock depends mainly on psychological factors. ("Treasury shares" here denotes both true treasury shares—those purchased on the open market some time prior to their delivery to the executive—and shares purchased on the open market and delivered directly to the executive. Both types cause the number of outstanding shares to remain unchanged, and therefore both are similar for executive compensation purposes.)

Some top managers become visibly upset when an executive sells even one of his company shares, even for tax purposes. These companies should stay away from all-stock payments, because they create a conflict for the individual executive: He is damned by the company if he sells the shares, and he is damned by IRS if he doesn't and defaults on his tax payments. These companies should also stay away from *any* stock payments, because giving an individual ostensibly convertible securities and then imposing psychological pressure to render them unconvertible sharply reduces the motivational value of the bonus itself. Indeed, the individual may eventually have to terminate his employment in order to gain the use of the money tied up in company stock. (There are also legal restrictions applicable to the sale of shares by certain executives, and these must also be considered.)

If authorized but unissued shares ("new shares") are utilized, the same psychological factors remain but an additional factor is introduced. New shares increase the number of shares outstanding and therefore cause a dilution in earnings per share. True, this dilution occurs at the time the shares are delivered to the individual and the act of sale is immaterial from an earnings-per-share standpoint. Even so, there is some evidence that company shareholders may be disturbed if there is a pattern of frequent sales. They feel, in effect, that the purpose of the plan has somehow been vitiated.

Nevertheless a company using new shares may elect to distribute the full bonus in company stock and risk shareholder dissatisfaction simply because it is strapped for cash. This is the only circumstance, in fact, in which the use of new shares would appear to be justified, because these shares have a double-barreled negative impact on earnings per share. First, the number of shares outstanding (the denominator in the earnings-per-share equation) is increased. Second, the after-tax earnings of the company (the numerator in the earnings-per-share equation) are reduced because of the deduction of the bonus amounts. On the other hand, the company not only has avoided laying out any cash, but has actually received additional cash flow, since, like depreciation of capital facilities and equipment, it obtains a deduction for the bonus payments but incurs no actual expenditure. When treasury shares are utilized, there is only one negative effect on earnings per share and that occurs in the numerator: The company's after-tax earnings are reduced because of the deduction of the bonus amounts.

Telling the Individual of His Award

The last step in the bonus procedure is, of course, to inform the individual that he has received an award. In many companies, this is accomplished in a letter signed by the president and sent to the individual's home. The recipient is probably addressed by his first name even if the president has never met him or spoken to him.

The reason advanced for this procedure is to give the bonus plan greater prestige. A letter from the president makes the executive feel that he is on the inside and a part of the true management team. This may be valid, but for the same reason, one would think that the president would personally communicate the rationale for *not* granting an award, if such were the case. Of course, this rarely happens—it is the immediate boss who is given the task of bearing bad tidings.

Chances are that the president communicates directly

with the award recipient to enhance not the bonus plan's prestige, but his personal prestige; after all, it's fun to play Santa Claus. Meanwhile, the president has undercut the individual's own supervisor, who made the initial recommendation that an award be granted, but may never have been informed as to the outcome. More than once, an executive, after receiving his award letter from the president, has gone to his boss to thank him, only to find that his boss was totally ignorant of the decision. ("Oh, so you got $10,000—well, that's just great!") After receiving such a reaction, the executive may well wonder if he should continue to look to his boss for his rewards. Some of the best "end runners" in the game of management first sharpened their skills on the company's bonus plan!

Some of the major principles involved in sound bonus plan design are these:

* Adopting meaningful award levels.
* Restricting regular eligibility to executives who have a *substantial* impact on the attainment of major company objectives.
* Providing for a few special awards to personnel not regularly eligible to participate.
* Designing an internal corporate funding formula to insure that the eligibles are motivated to accomplish what the company really wants accomplished.
* Designing an external corporate funding formula to act as a circuit breaker on the internal formula and assure the shareholders that amounts expended on executive bonuses will always be reasonable and in line with the company's ability to pay.

* Developing allocation procedures which recognize that some units outperform others. Better yet, designing individual unit internal funding formulas to generate part of the funds for that unit.
* Using the total integrated compensation range to establish bonus amounts, rather than paying bonuses as a percentage of base salary.
* Appraising executive performance realistically. Recognizing that in virtually every company there have to be some below average executives and seeing to it that they receive no awards.
* Always trying to grant outstanding personnel the award they deserve without regard to the size of the fund itself. Recognizing that dollars used to pay even token awards to mediocre executives usually come out of the pockets of the outstanding ones.

6

Deferred Compensation

Deferred compensation, as its name implies, is compensation earned in one year but paid in some future year. In its fullest application, deferred compensation covers payments made under company retirement, profit-sharing, and savings plans and even the payment of postretirement medical expenses. (Life insurance is of course the ultimate in deferred compensation!) This chapter, however, is restricted to the types of deferred compensation that are typically granted only to executive personnel. In tax parlance, these devices come under the label of nonqualified deferred compensation plans.

Deferred compensation for executives usually takes one of three forms: salary deferrals, bonus deferrals, or an employment agreement which provides for supplementary retirement payments (in addition to those provided under the company's qualified retirement, profit-sharing, or savings plans). Since bonus deferrals contain the greatest variety of design options, the greater part of this chapter has been given over to a detailed discussion of these deferrals.

Bonus Deferrals

Bonus deferrals can be grouped into two categories: short-term deferrals and long-term deferrals. Short-term deferrals involve paying part of the award at the time it is declared, with the remainder to be paid over the next few years. For example, a $10,000 award may be paid in five equal annual installments, consisting of $2,000 immediately and $2,000 in each of the next four years. The number of years that various companies use in their deferral cycles ranges from two to five. It should be noted, however, that the four- and five-year deferral cycles are the most common.

Long-term deferrals involve the postponement of the entire award until retirement or other termination of employment. Thereafter, the award is again typically paid in a series of equal annual installments, but in this case the deferral cycle is usually longer. Ten- to fifteen-year cycles are the most common.

Both motivational and tax reasons are cited as advantages of deferred compensation. (Tax reasons can of course be considered motivational if the executive yields more after-tax income, but for discussion purposes they are considered separately.) Let us now take a look at the evidence.

Golden Handcuffs Revisited

As was stated earlier, the golden handcuffs approach is a negatively oriented motivational device which does not give the executive an incentive to remain with the company but rather gives him a "disincentive" to leave the company. The late social psychologist Kurt Lewin developed an ingenious "field theory" of motivation around principles operating in the physical world. He postulated that at any given point in time the individual is surrounded by both positive and negative motivational vectors and that the relative strength of these vectors dictates the direction in which the individual moves. Thus, if the positive vectors outweigh the negative ones, the individual moves in the direction indicated by the positive forces. Similarly, he would move in the direction of the negative vectors if they were the stronger. The theory also posits that the individual remains immobilized if the positive and negative forces are equal. An interesting thing happened in some experiments, however. When the individual was confronted with both positive and negative forces of known and equal physical intensity, he did not remain immobilized but moved toward the positive force. In effect, the individual had a "set" to evaluate the positive forces as being worth more psychologically than physically.

So it may also be with money and deferred compensation. If a man is confronted with a positive force in the form of an offer from another company which will buy him out of the money he will lose by quitting and a negative force in the form of the golden handcuffs approach, he may well move to the other company even though the dollars involved are merely equal to and not more than he is losing. Moreover, in this instance he is subject to another psychological phenomenon—the grass is greener—and this may impel an even quicker movement in the "positive" direction.

Thus a company that wants to make a negatively oriented motivational device like golden handcuffs really work may find itself having to use an even greater amount of money than it otherwise might. But this is the start of a vicious circle, for the greater the deferred compensation, the easier it is to motivate the individual to accept an offer from another company. This is because his cash flow income is less than his nominal income, as mentioned earlier. For example, an executive with a base salary of $50,000 and a $25,000 bonus in five equal annual installments receives only $55,000 total cash flow during the first year of such an arrangement. He is obviously vulnerable to another company's offer of $75,000 with no deferrals. In the reverse situation, the company finds it difficult to attract a talented executive from a company which pays immediate cash bonuses.

Although the evidence on the efficacy of golden handcuffs is sparse, what does exist is not very encouraging. Some companies have tried and then abandoned the golden handcuffs approach, because it failed to retain outstanding personnel. In other companies, golden handcuffs are used with a vengeance. The air is heavy with the threat of discharge, and discharge, in these companies, carries a forfeiture of all unpaid deferred compensation installments. It is no coincidence that executives in these companies are characterized by passivity and an unwillingness to make gutty decisions that offer the possibility of becoming a hero, but also offer an equal possibility of being discharged at great financial sacrifice.

One claimed motivational advantage of golden handcuffs is its ability, in a short-term deferral application, to equalize an executive's income from year to year. This was an advantage years ago when short-term deferrals first got started in American industry, but it may not be an advantage any longer.

Credit for initiating short-term deferrals is generally given to the automobile industry, which is characterized by huge bonuses relative to base salary and substantial fluctuations in year-to-year profits. Thus bonuses that are huge one year may be minuscule the next. And, if a bonus is paid consistently for some years, executives come to depend on at least part of it to maintain their standard of living.

Without an income-averaging provision in the tax laws, as was the case prior to 1964, the payment of a huge bonus one year and a small bonus the next was terribly inefficient from a tax standpoint because the huge bonus was hit with extremely high marginal tax rates (up to 91 percent in those days). Thus, when it was first initiated, the short-term deferral cycle made a good deal of sense.

Today, we have both an income-averaging provision and a lower marginal income tax rate. Together, these protect the executive who receives varying total compensation from year to year. Moreover, most industries neither pay bonus awards of the magnitude of the auto industry nor experience quite the same degree of year-to-year profit fluctuation.

In fact, there is one school of thought which argues that short-term deferrals, through their year-to-year equalization of income, actually provide diminished motivation because they dilute the impact of an exceptionally good year followed by an exceptionally poor one. For example, the individual who receives a $25,000 bonus in each of four years under a five-year short-term deferral will still receive $20,000 in the fifth year, even if he receives no new awards that year because his performance is poor. Conversely, if his performance is superb, and his bonus in the fifth year is doubled to $50,000, his cash flow that year will be only $30,000—$20,000 from his previous four bonuses and the first installment of $10,000 from his current bonus. Thus the difference between superb and poor performance is a cash flow of $30,000 versus $20,000, not $50,000 versus zero, as in the nominal bonus amounts.

Although it is true that no one has proved that the short-term deferral approach diminishes motivation, it is equally true that the advantages of equalizing income from year to year are lost after a number of years in the company's deferral cycle. Thus an individual who receives a $25,000 bonus for five years under a five-cycle short-term deferral receives $25,000 cash flow in the sixth year and each year thereafter as long as he continues to receive additional $25,000 awards. His cash flow compensation then equals his nominal compensation, and little further advantage accrues from the use of short-term deferrals.

This does not necessarily mean that the company should not employ any holding devices. Some executives—particularly the younger ones—may indulge in impulsive behavior which they later regret. A modest amount of holding power may therefore be desirable to curb these impulsive acts and at least make the executive think twice. But such holding power is already supplied by forfeiture provisions in the company's retirement, profit-sharing, and savings plans and by benefits that are related to length of service, such as vacations. These are enough to make one think.

It is correct to say that a person is *motivated* to hand over his wallet to someone holding a gun on him. The same sort of negative motivation is implied by the golden handcuffs approach. An alternative approach, designed to stress the symbiotic aspects of the employee-employer relationship, obviously therefore seems to be far more preferable.

Perhaps the best way to summarize the arguments against golden handcuffs is to recount the experience one company president had when, at the annual stockholders meeting, he introduced a new bonus plan incorporating this feature. He gave an impassioned speech extolling the virtues of the new plan and said it would materially aid the company in attracting and especially in retaining capable executives. When he was finished, one of the world's most famous dissident stockholders rose and said, "Mr. President, I have listened to your remarks with great interest and am happy to learn how your new plan will attract and retain capable executives. Now, sitting three places from your left is an individual whom my proxy statement identifies as Mr. Jones. He is a vice-president of your company and president of its XYZ division. Mr. President, if I recall, I first saw Mr. Jones at the annual meeting of the ABC company some four years ago. He was a vice-president of that company and was being paid a large deferred bonus to attract and retain him. Then about two years ago, Mr. President, I again saw Mr. Jones. This time he was vice-president of the DEF Company and was again being paid a large deferred bonus to attract and retain him. I have only one question, Mr. President. Where will Mr. Jones be two years from now?"

It is a good question.

Individualization of Deferrals

Individualization of the compensation package is one good answer. Here, the individual is not made to take something he doesn't want but instead is offered the chance to take something he definitely wants. Obviously, if he decides to defer some or all of his bonus, no strings should be attached to his choice; and he should be permitted to receive *all* his funds when he resigns—whatever the reason. Since the executive will probably choose the type of compensation which is most appealing to him at that particular moment—and hence highly motivating—and since not every company is employing the individualization approach, its use can give a company a significant edge over the competition in attracting, retaining, and motivating executive personnel.

Tax Consequences of Short-Term Deferrals

Now let us turn to the tax consequences of short-term deferrals. Ostensibly, the executive gains a tax advantage by spreading his bonus over a number of years and thereby equalizing his income. The top slice of this income will presumably attract a lower marginal ordinary income tax rate than a large bonus all in one year.

There are several factors working against such an advantage, however. First, as noted earlier, there is an income-averaging provision in the current income tax law, and this helps the executive avoid the higher taxes associated with unusual swings in total compensation. Second, since the payment installments under a short-term deferral are made while the individual is still employed, and since his salary is unlikely to go in any direction but up, the executive may well find himself paying a higher marginal tax rate on the last few installments of any award than would have been the case had he received it in a lump sum.

Third, tax rates themselves have shown a distinct, if not discomfiting, tendency to rise. Certainly, there was the much-heralded reduction of federal income taxes in 1964 (much heralded because there had never been a tax reduction before). Yet there was a distinct tendency for state and local income taxes to rise and fill the void. To the extent that tax rates rise, the value of deferring income will be offset.

Fourth, if the deferred monies are not invested, the individual is certain to suffer a penalty from short-term deferrals. After all, he could have taken the monies immediately, paid his taxes on them, put them to work. Surprisingly, there are many companies with short-term deferral plans that do not invest the money being held for future distribution. For them, such an approach is a good deal, and in fact they may be able to earn enough on the retained capital to pay for the entire cost of the last few installments. For the individual executive, however, such an approach is no deal at all.

Fifth and finally, a revolutionary development has been introduced by the Tax Reform Act of 1969. For the first time, different tax rates have been established for "earned income," such as salary and bonuses, and other income, such as interest and dividends from investments. Earned income, starting in 1972, will be taxable at a maximum marginal rate of 50 percent, while other ordinary income will continue to be taxed at the previous rates. Deferred compensation will be considered earned income only when it is paid prior to the end of the tax year following the year in which it is no longer subject to substantial risk of forfeiture. This provision therefore requires the use of golden hand-cuffs. The company that uses it must adopt a negatively oriented motivational device and forgo the positive advantages accruing from making a free and individualized choice.

Much is lost, and the only thing that is gained is the ability to pay taxes on deferred compensation at the same rates that would have applied had no deferred compensation been adopted in the first place. Thus the case for a tax advantage with the use of short-term deferrals appears to be built on shifting sands.

To the company, the tax consequences of short-term deferrals are rather simple. The company can deduct deferred amounts only when they are actually paid to the individual. Thus the company must postpone its tax deduction vis-à-vis a lump sum payment. The only problem that may arise is that the company may be forced to take a deduction in the year in which it least wants to take one. When income is very low, the last thing the company may want to do is lower it still further.

Tax Consequences of Long-Term Deferrals

A more compelling case can be made for the tax advantages of long-term deferrals, but the road is uncertain in this area also.

The reason most often advanced as to why long-term deferrals are advantageous is that the individual will probably be earning less after retirement and thus will have a lower marginal tax bracket for additional ordinary income. (Deferred amounts are generally taxed at ordinary rates based on their value as of the time of payment.) Hence, deferred amounts taken after retirement have a good chance of being taxed at a lower rate than would be the case had they been received immediately. Again, there are several pitfalls in this argument.

First, the test as to whether tax rates are indeed lower must be made between the year in which the bonus was initially declared and the year in which the installment is received—not between the last year of employment and the first year of retirement. On this basis, it may turn out that the individual has no tax advantage at all. For example, suppose a man with a $30,000 salary had some bonus money deferred until after his retirement. Suppose further that the company has a final-pay retirement plan which provides a benefit equal to 50 percent of the last year's salary. If the deferral occurred early in the man's career and his salary had meanwhile advanced to $80,000 per year, he would retire with annual payments of $40,000 per year from the retirement plan and would thus be in a higher bracket for additional ordinary income than he was way back in the year in which the money was first deferred.

Then, too, there is the matter of outside income. This obviously has a tendency to rise as the individual grows older and hence may represent a significant portion of his postretirement income. Because of this, the individual actually has to be receiving substantially lower company retirement income when the installment is paid than he received in salary when the award was first declared before there can be any advantage at all.

The impact of tax rates and tax laws on deferrals should not be overlooked. Long-term deferrals involve a long period of time, during which taxes will probably rise. The extent of the rise will determine whether long-term deferrals will be seriously eroded. And if Congress should act to change the rules governing deferred compensation, this could deal an especially serious blow to long-term deferrals, which depend heavily for their tax efficacy on the assumption that the individual's tax rates will be reduced.

Government Tax Money as Investment Capital

There is, however, one very important tax advantage to deferred compensation, and this is the executive's ability to use government tax money—the amounts he would have paid as taxes had he taken the income immediately—as investment capital. Assume, for example, that a 45-year-old executive who received a $50,000 bonus immediately would have to turn over 50 percent of it—or $25,000—to the government. (As noted, a maximum tax rate of 50 percent will apply to earned income after 1972.) He would be left with $25,000 which he could invest. Assume further that he invests his $25,000 in such a way that he receives no dividends or interest for the 20 years prior to his retirement but does increase his original investment to $100,000—a fourfold appreciation. He therefore has a long-term capital gain of $75,000.

Assume again that the executive's marginal tax bracket for additional ordinary income drops to 40 percent after his retirement and that he sells only a portion of his investment each year. Therefore, he can expect to be taxed at a rate of only 20 percent on long-term capital gains and can keep at least 80 percent of his total appreciation. His after-tax proceeds will therefore be $85,000, consisting of his original $25,000 investment and 80 percent of his $75,000 appreciation.

Suppose, however, the original award of $50,000 was deferred and invested in the very same securities. No tax is payable until the securities are handed over to the executive, and therefore the entire $50,000 is put to work. Since it was invested in the same securities, it will also quadruple in value, appreciating to a total of $200,000 by the time the executive retires. The full value of these securities is taxable at ordinary income tax rates when distributed to the individual, but, by taking it over a period of time, he can hope to maintain a 40 to 50 percent postretirement bracket for additional ordinary income. Thus he stands to retain 50 to 60 percent of the $200,000 of deferred compensation—or $100,000 to $120,000. This represents a very substantial increase over the $85,000 he would have received by paying his taxes at once and going for a long-term capital gain.

Even the 1969 proposal to tax some deferred compensation payments at the rates in effect when they were first declared would not have totally defeated this important advantage of using government tax money, although a check of individual circumstances would have had to be made.

The use of government tax money as investment capital presupposes, of course, that the deferred compensation will be invested. Surprisingly, a good many companies do not invest deferred compensation, or if they do, they do not give the executive the benefit of any appreciation. Thus the $10,000 that is deferred when the executive is age 40 is the same $10,000 that will be paid him after he reaches age 65. Meanwhile, tax rates may have risen, and the executive will have lost the opportunity to put his money to work. During the same period, inflation, which is seemingly endemic in this country, will have had plenty of time to work its special magic on the purchasing power of the original $10,000. Therefore, unless deferred compensation is invested, the executive not only is not better off, but is far worse off than he would have been if he had taken the money immediately.

Investment Media

There is no single investment medium for deferred compensation funds that is best for everyone, but the length of time involved in long-term deferrals suggests the use of some sort of equity security to provide protection against the ravages of inflation. Some companies use fixed income securities, and others guarantee the individual the same rate of interest on his funds as the company itself pays to borrow money. But the most common practice among those who do invest deferred compensation monies is to place them in company stock. Being an equity security, company stock seemingly protects against inflation and may offer some additional on-the-job motivation—the executive is naturally interested in protecting his investment.

The only problem with company stock is that the executive, what with his stock options and his profit-sharing and savings plan proceeds, runs the risk of becoming "company stock poor." In terms of sound investment practice, such an event is undesirable in any company; in some companies it is particularly undesirable, because the company's stock cannot, by the wildest stretch of anyone's imagination, be considered to have the stability that characterizes a sound long-term growth vehicle.

As a result of these problems with company stock, a few companies offer their executives an opportunity to place deferred compensation monies in equities of other issuers, either in a diversified portfolio selected by company officers or the company's bank or in a mutual fund. From an investment standpoint, this sort of opportunity makes a good deal of sense, especially when it is coupled with at least some amount of company stock. On the other hand, some company presidents fear that such an approach will bring a withering blast of criticism from the shareholders, who may feel that management, through its purchase of equities of other issuers, has vividly demonstrated its lack of confidence in its own stock.

If outside securities are selected by management, there is the further problem that the company will be blamed for investment losses or will at the least be subject to the deprecations of Monday morning quarterbacks. Most companies use outside advice for this reason.

Deferred Compensation Contracts

Sometimes, instead of being geared to the company's bonus plan, deferred compensation takes the form of individual executive contracts which specify that certain postretirement payments be made. Usually these contracts provide that the executive must actually retire from the company ("If you remain until retirement, you will receive $25,000 per year for the remainder of your life") or are geared to his length of service ("For each year of service, you will receive a single payment of $25,000 after your retirement"). In addition, it is common practice to require that the executive, as a condition of receiving the money, either refrain from joining a competitor after his

191

retirement, or hold himself available as a consultant, or both. These conditions are golden handcuffs of a sort, but they are so relatively mild as to be insignificant. It is rare that an executive would join a competitor after his retirement; and, if he never seems to be available for consultation, the company probably wouldn't object because it is not likely to call him anyway!

These conditions are essentially included to avoid any conflict with the IRS doctrine of constructive receipt, which is discussed shortly. It is ironic, however, that use of the consulting requirement in particular has caused IRS in some cases to claim that the individual's deferred compensation payments represent income from gainful employment (consulting), hence unwittingly invalidating the executive's claim to social security benefits.

For all practical purposes, therefore, the deferred compensation contained in individual employment contracts is not substantially different from that obtained under a bonus plan, except that the latter form of compensation may, if the plan is soundly designed, be better related to the individual's performance than the former, which ultimately represents compensation for staying alive and out of trouble.

Tax Consequences to the Company

As with short-term deferrals, the company does not receive a tax deduction on long-term deferred compensation payments until they are actually made. At that time, the company can deduct the full value of the payment, including all appreciation above the original amount deferred. (Of course, if the value has declined below the original amount contributed, the company loses part of its deduction.)

Accounting reserves can be established for deferred compensation monies but they cannot be formally funded, with payments guaranteed to the executive by some agency outside the company. A few companies tried to establish deferred trusts for their executives, but IRS held that such a company was not entitled to a deduction at the time the money was deposited in the trust, because the trust was not an employee. Moreover, the company was also denied a deduction at the time the monies were actually paid to the executive, because they were technically paid by the trust and not the company. Furthermore, if a trust was established and no conditions were imposed on the ultimate transfer of the monies to the executive, he would have immediate income and would be taxed on it as such.

Therefore, deferred compensation monies must remain unfunded, so they constitute a sort of lien on the company. Since a considerable amount of money can be built up over the years, and since the company may not always be able to anticipate when payments are to be made (for example, if the individual resigns prior to retirement, and no golden handcuffs restrictions have been imposed; or if he dies), the company might have to take a deduction in the very year when it could least afford it. This is probably not a major problem for most companies, but it should at least be noted before adopting a deferred compensation plan.

Individualizing the Deferred Compensation Plan

As noted earlier, a more motivational approach to deferred compensation is to let each eligible executive decide what he wants to do with his money and, if he elects to defer it, to grant him that election without imposing golden handcuffs restrictions.

As an example, the executive might elect to defer what subsequently turns out to be a $10,000 bonus. In addition to specifying the portion of his bonus to be deferred, the executive might also be allowed to choose the manner in which the deferred funds were to be invested (bonds, company stock, or a mutual fund) and the disposition of dividends and interest (either payment to him as declared or reinvestment in the media from which the monies were generated). Finally, he might also choose the year in which the repayment of the deferred monies (plus any appreciation thereon) would commence and the number of annual installments in which the entire amount would be paid.

A plan of this type does involve some administrative expense, but it is usually only a tiny fraction of the total amount being deferred. And, since the executive is receiving the types of compensation he prefers, the potential motivational benefits to be derived from an individualized approach far outweigh the meager costs involved.

The Doctrine of Constructive Receipt

The types of choices just described, while highly motivational, will be self-defeating if the executive has to pay full and immediate taxes on his entire award at the time it is declared. This will be the penalty if the company or the executive runs afoul of the IRS doctrine of constructive receipt. In effect, an individual is presumed to have income at any time he can—to quote IRS—"reach out his hand and take it." Thus, if the company were to say to the executive,

"You're going to receive a $10,000 award; what do you want to do with it?" and the executive were to reply, "Defer it," the money would be duly deferred. But meanwhile, the executive would have to ante up the taxes on the entire award by the next April 15. When the company announced the bonus, he could have taken it, and the fact that he didn't is immaterial because as IRS also says, "A taxpayer cannot turn his back voluntarily on income."

The doctrine of constructive receipt, like the Monroe Doctrine, is conceptually clear but not always easy to apply. As a result, some time ago IRS published five case histories to illustrate which types of deferred compensation would breach the doctrine of constructive receipt and which would not. While IRS's intentions were entirely honorable, it only added to the confusion, for there seemed to be no discernible logic running through all five of the case histories. As an additional "service," therefore, it consented to make advance rulings on deferred compensation plans.

Although there are no hard and fast rules in the area of constructive receipt, it does appear that an executive can voluntarily defer compensation payments if he elects to do so sufficiently in advance of the time when the compensation is actually earned. It is even more helpful if the executive, at the time he makes the election, is uncertain as to what the compensation will eventually be. Thus, on January 1, at least one year prior to the date of a bonus award, the executive might give the company a statement that reads: "I don't know whether I am going to receive a bonus 14 months from now, and, if I do receive one, I don't know what the amount will be, but should a bonus be awarded to me, I would like to defer 75 percent of it until my retirement or other termination of employment."

Generally speaking, the more time between the date an

election to defer is filed and the date the compensation is actually earned, the less likely it is that the executive will encounter problems with the Internal Revenue Service.

Because of the uncertainties surrounding the doctrine of constructive receipt, a company considering an individualized deferred compensation plan should never venture forth without a Bible in one hand and a very competent tax lawyer in the other.

Personal Financial Planning

Contrary to many executives' implicit beliefs, there has not been an automatic tax advantage to deferred compensation payments for many years. The Tax Reform Act of 1969, with its provision of a 50 percent maximum rate on earned income but not on freely chosen deferrals muddies the waters still further. And now we have a number of progressive companies granting the executive options as to how his compensation is to be paid.

Unless he is a tax lawyer how can the executive make an intelligent choice? For that matter, how is he going to find sufficient time to manage his outside investments, considering the ever increasing demands of his company? The sad result is that many executives, even those concerned with company finance, neglect their own personal financial planning and miss significant opportunities to increase their net worth.

These executives do not lack for advice, but unfortunately most of it is somewhat biased. The mutual fund salesman or the life insurance salesman will be only too happy to perform a detailed analysis of the executive's personal finances, but the recommendations will more than likely involve healthy investments in mutual funds or life insurance.

As a result, separate companies or specialized sections of consulting firms have recently been created to help the executive in his personal financial planning. Groups of experts skilled in various types of investments analyze the executive's total financial picture and provide him with unbiased advice. The advice is truly unbiased because the fee for this service depends on the total assets being analyzed; these groups do not receive brokerage fees, life insurance commissions, or the like.

Some companies pay for this type of service, because they see it as a cheap way of obtaining more of the executive's time and energy. And because an outside service is involved, the company can stay out of the executive's personal financial affairs.

Properly designed deferred compensation plans can have both motivational and tax advantages. But neither advantage is automatic. Deferred compensation in particular is likely to motivate only to the extent that it appeals to the individual executive. Even the most clear-cut tax advantage is worth little if the executive has an urgent need for current income. Yet there are few clear-cut tax advantages in the area of deferred compensation.

Therefore two basic principles should be followed in making intelligent use of deferred compensation:

1. Carefully analyze the tax consequences—both to the individual and to the company—of various deferred

compensation alternatives. Never assume that, just because other companies have adopted a given practice, it is necessarily tax-advantageous.

2. Give the executive a choice. Don't force him to take deferred compensation—no matter how advantageous it may appear. And, above all, don't adopt the golden handcuffs approach, for it is likely to motivate the wrong people into staying with the company.

7

Stock Options

THERE are three major types of stock option plans: (1) qualified stock options, (2) nonqualified stock options, and (3) "phantom" stock options. Let us consider these options and their tax consequences to the individual executive.

Qualified Stock Options

A qualified stock option plan is one which "qualifies" for favorable tax treatment, provided that certain conditions are met:

★ The plan must be approved by the shareholders, and the total number of shares reserved for options over the life of the plan must be specified.

* The plan must expire no later than ten years after it is first adopted.

* The option price per share must be at least equal to the fair market value of the stock as of the date any grant is made.

* An individual option must be exercised within five years from its date of grant.

* The optionee must be an employee of the company and, after the grant has been made, may not own more than 5 percent of the total shares outstanding. (This rule has been somewhat liberalized for very small companies.)

* The optionee may not exercise an option so long as another qualified option granted on an earlier date and carrying a higher option price per share is currently outstanding.

Provided that an option meets all these conditions (and a few minor conditions as well) and provided that the executive holds his stock for at least three years after its exercise, he will, when he eventually sells the shares, qualify for long-term capital gains tax treatment on all appreciation which has occurred above the original option price.

The option "spread." For discussion, it is helpful to divide the total appreciation that may occur in an option transaction into two parts. The first is the difference between the option price and the market value of the stock as of the date of exercise. The "spread" (as this part is called) is what makes an option worthwhile, for it represents risk-free appreciation and an effective discount in the price of the stock that is not available to the ordinary investor. The second portion of appreciation is the gain in the stock's market value that occurs after the option has been exercised but prior to its sale. This portion represents no special advantage for the optionee, for he could obtain it as an ordinary investor simply by purchasing the stock on the open market on the date of exercise.

If the optionee does not hold his stock for at least three years after its exercise and thereby makes what is known as a disqualifying disposition, he must pay ordinary tax rates on the spread. The second portion of appreciation, however, is taxable as long-term capital gains if he has held the stock for at least six months. (This advantage is also available to the ordinary investor.)

Option plans qualified by IRS to receive special tax advantages have become substantially more restrictive since the 1964 revenue act was passed. Prior to that, companies were permitted to grant what were known as restricted stock options (not to be confused with grants and options of restricted stock, which had a great appeal for a limited time).

These earlier options could be granted for a ten-year period and at an option price as low as 85 percent of the market value as of the time of grant. Moreover, if the individual held the stock for only six months, he could qualify for long-term capital gains tax treatment on almost all the appreciation between the market value on the date of grant and the eventual sales price. Thus, in 1964, Congress substantially diminished the appeal of IRS-qualified stock option plans. In one blow, option terms were halved, minimum option prices rose 17 percent, and the holding period sextupled.

Provisions imposed by the company. Qualified stock option plans often contain additional provisions imposed, not as a matter of law, but by the company. For example, a given option grant may not be exercised immediately; 25

percent of the total number of shares can be exercised (on a cumulative basis) on each of the first four anniversaries succeeding the date of the grant. Such features are known as delayed exercise provisions.

Nonqualified Stock Option Plans

In defining a nonqualified option plan, it is easier to say what the plan is not than what it is. In essence, a nonqualified option plan is one which contains one or more provisions (or lacks one or more provisions) which render it incapable of becoming a qualified stock option plan. The option price may be less than the market value as of the date of grant. Or the option may extend for a term of more than five years. Or the plan may have the same features as a qualified stock option plan but simply may not be approved by the shareholders.

With a nonqualified option plan, the optionee is taxed on the spread at ordinary income tax rates in the year of exercise. After the stock has been held for at least six months, any additional appreciation is taxable as long-term capital gains.

Phantom Stock Plans

A phantom stock option is a special type of nonqualified stock option. Under a plan of this type, the executive is granted a number of units, each of which entitles him to a payment equal to any appreciation that occurs in the market value of a share of company stock between the date of the grant and some future date (most typically, a date five years later). As with the other types of stock option

plans, the executive receives risk-free appreciation for a
period of time. Unlike the other plans, however, he does
not have to make any investments of his own; nor does he
have any choice as to when he will exercise his option.

Any compensation payable under a phantom stock
option plan is taxable to the executive as ordinary income
in the year in which such compensation is paid. This rule
applies whether the payments are made in cash (the usual
practice) or in company stock (the number of shares of
which is typically determined by dividing the dollars involved by the market price of the stock as of the date of
payment).

Advantages Attributed to Options

Stock options are purported to have a number of important advantages. First, they appear to offer longer-range
motivation than is contained in the typical executive bonus
plan, which is usually predicated on the current year's results. (One company adopted a nonqualified option plan
with ten-year option terms to gain an even longer-range
motivation.) Second, they link at least part of the executive's rewards to those of the shareholders, thereby providing the basis for a symbiotic relationship and presumably
encouraging a greater degree of entrepreneurial behavior.

Third, options can be a relatively invisible compensation
device, provided that the option price is at least equal to the
market value of the stock on the date of the grant (which
of course must be the case with a qualified stock option).
In this manner, the value of the option, at least when it is
granted, is impossible to ascertain; and the value that later
accrues to the optionee when the market value of the stock

begins to rise is, for some reason, largely forgotten. Non-qualified option plans which undercut the market price of the stock as of the date of the grant are obviously more visible compensation devices, the amount of visibility being proportional to the discount.

Fourth, stock options represent what is perhaps the prime executive status symbol. Being granted an option is roughly analogous to being accepted for membership in a very exclusive country club. Moreover, options have been so glamorized in the press that even the neighbors are likely to treat the optionee with renewed respect. Thus options contain a significant amount of recognition (or psychic income).

Fifth, and finally, qualified stock options (in contrast to other types of options) provide the executive with potential tax advantages. Although the tax advantages of qualified options are here listed last, many top executives see them as most important, which accounts for a good part of their popularity. (The impact of the Tax Reform Act of 1969 on qualified stock options is discussed in Chapter 8.)

And they are certainly popular! In one recent study, better than 80 percent of companies listed on the New York Stock Exchange had a qualified stock option plan. Nonqualified stock option plans are much less popular, and phantom stock option plans are rare, but are becoming more popular for reasons discussed shortly. Let us now turn to some of the design features of qualified stock option plans.

Eligibility

The size of the stock option eligible group varies widely —and wildly—among companies. Some companies give virtually every employee an option—even the janitors. On the other end of the spectrum, the eligible group may consist of only five to ten top executives. Part of the reason for this wide variance is the great secrecy with which companies typically surround their stock option plans. Although companies exchange base salary and bonus information quite freely, for some reason they are loath to talk about their option plans. As noted earlier, the exchange of compensation information through surveys has given feedback and has caused companies at the extremes to move toward the average. There has been no comparable feedback in the area of stock options.

Statistically speaking, however, the average company includes far fewer executives for stock option eligibility than for bonus eligibility. In one study of 13 large companies, the smallest of which had 30,000 employees, the average number of eligibles was 236, and the average percentage of total population covered for eligibility was 0.3 percent. In the same group of companies, bonus eligibility, on the other hand, typically averaged one percent of total population.

When the motivational problems associated with stock options are discussed in the next chapter, more is said about the executives who should be eligible for stock options.

Size of Grants

The relationship between the size of stock option grants and base salary is similar to the relationship between bonuses and base salary described earlier. In effect, as the salary rises, the size of the grant rises even faster. This is illustrated in Exhibit 4, which is based on a Booz, Allen &

Hamilton Inc. survey of 450 executives in a variety of companies. In this exhibit, stock option grants during a five-year period have been converted into a multiple of base salary and then related to the executive's base salary. To illustrate, suppose an executive whose salary was $50,000 received one option during a five-year period consisting of 4,000 shares at an option price of $50 per share. The size of his option was therefore $200,000 (4,000 times $50), and his option as a multiple of his base salary was 4.0 ($200,000 divided by $50,000). If the executive had received not one but several options during the five-year period under study, the separate options would have been added together and the resulting figure divided by the original base salary to establish the multiple.

Exhibit 4 **Relationship of qualified stock option grants to base salary.**

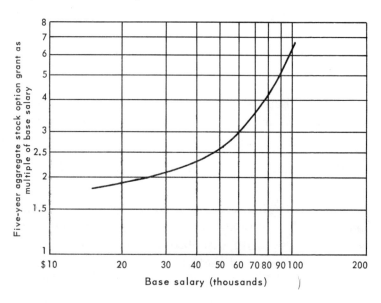

It can be seen from this exhibit that the option multiple increases as the salary increases. Thus an individual with a base salary of $25,000 per year is, on the average, likely to receive twice his salary—or $50,000—in option stock during a five-year period. On the other hand, an executive with a base salary of $100,000 is, on the average, likely to receive seven times his salary—or $700,000—in option stock during a five-year period.

As with option eligibility, option sizes vary greatly around the average. Thus individual multiples making up the average of 2.0 times salary at the $25,000 salary level ranged from 1.1 to 4.9 times base salary. Similarly, the multiples making up the average of 6.8 times salary at the $100,-000 salary level ranged from 3.0 to 14.5 times salary. Again, this variance is very likely a product of the infrequency of option surveys among companies.

The size of stock options is therefore quite considerable —especially at the higher salary levels. Size, however, does not necessarily translate into income for the optionee—even $1 million of option stock can be worth only $500,000 in five years. Nevertheless, the size of the grant defines the opportunity for appreciation and is therefore of considerable importance.

Frequency of Grants

Stock option grants, unlike base salary payments and bonus awards, are not necessarily made each year. Until recently, in fact, the usual practice was to make large grants at infrequent intervals—for example, once every five years.

More frequent—usually annual—grants are being used more often, and for good reasons. First, an annual grant permits dollar averaging of option prices. Normally, this would be considered a disadvantage, but, with qualified option plans, an individual cannot exercise a more recent option at a lower price until he has first exercised (or allowed to expire) an option granted earlier at a higher price. Thus a large grant of option stock at what later turns out to be a spuriously high option price can effectively exclude an individual from the plan for up to five years. With smaller grants, the individual is at least given the opportunity to nibble away at digestible portions of high-priced stock to get at a more appetizing but later grant.

Second, the use of annual option grants allows a better balance between grants and performance. (It sometimes happens that an individual who receives a large grant fails to live up to his initial promise.) Annual grants also give the executive the feeling that the company hasn't forgotten him—the "what have you done for me lately?" syndrome.

When coupled with delayed exercise provisions, annual grants also offer a degree of holding power, and on a less negatively oriented basis than the golden handcuffs approach used in bonus plans. For example, suppose a company combines annual grants with a provision that makes 50 percent of the option exercisable on the first anniversary of the grant and the second 50 percent (plus any portion of the first 50 percent not yet exercised) on the second anniversary of the grant. With this approach, no more than 70 percent of an executive's option stock will be exercisable at any given point in time; and 30 percent of his stock will be subject to forfeiture in the event of his termination. (Of five consecutive annual grants, all equal in size, three will be fully exercisable, one will be 50 percent exercisable, and the most recent will not be exercisable; hence the 70 percent figure just mentioned.) Unlike the golden handcuffs approach in bonus awards, the executive is not faced with giving up something he has already gained, but with losing something he never had in the first place.

Smaller, more frequent option grants also seem to be preferred by individual executives. In the Booz, Allen & Hamilton survey, some 57 percent of the respondents indicated this preference.

Granting Guidelines

Too often, decisions regarding option grants are extremely casual. When the president thinks about it (perhaps when he himself has run out of option stock), he will consider making additional grants to his subordinates. After a hurried and superficial performance assessment, grants are made, usually involving multiples of 500 shares—which, after all, are nice even numbers. Of course, if the stock happens to be priced in the IBM range, a mistake of 500 shares could result in an error of about $150,000.

A better approach is to establish annual granting multiples for various levels of executives and apply these to each executive's targeted total compensation. For example, the average granting multiple over a five-year period for an executive with a $40,000 base salary is 2.3 times base salary. (See Exhibit 4.) Suppose a company had adopted the five-point integrated total compensation structure discussed in Chapter 2, and suppose the total compensation control point corresponding to a salary control point of $40,000 was $52,-000, reflecting the average 30 percent bonus that companies typically pay at this salary level. Dividing the 2.3 base salary multiple for a five-year period by 1.30 (the average bonus percentage) converts it into a 1.77 total compensation multiple for a five-year period. Dividing the 1.77 multiple by 5 permits a further conversion to an annual multiple. The resulting figure, which is then applied to total cash compensation, is 0.35.

Let us examine this procedure in practice. An average executive in our hypothetical position will earn a $40,000 salary per year, which represents the salary control point in his range. Since he is average, he will receive a bonus of $12,000, giving him total cash compensation of $52,000, which represents the total compensation control point of his range. The annual stock option granting guideline of 0.35 will then be applied to his total cash compensation of $52,000 to produce an option grant of $18,200 (which is then converted into option shares by dividing by the current market value of the company's stock). Five such grants over a five-year period (assuming that his total compensation remains unchanged) will therefore produce an aggregate option grant of $91,000, which after all is said and done represents 2.3 times his base salary of $40,000—or the starting point from which these guidelines were derived.

Why go through such a complicated procedure? There are two distinct advantages. First, option guidelines have been established to insure that the company remains competitive in its granting practices and that higher-level executives receive proportionally more stock. Second, the executive's demonstrated performance is allowed to play a key role in determining option size. This performance is measured by the targeted position in the total compensation range that has been assigned to the executive; and it is to this targeted position that the granting guideline is applied. Thus, while the granting guideline remains unchanged, the size of the grant is allowed to vary according to individual performance through the use of various targeted range positions. In this manner, the proper amount of stock is granted, in terms of both competitive factors and performance contributions.

This recommended approach must, however, be considered only a guideline. There will undoubtedly be occasions when more or less stock than that provided by the guideline should be granted; and in such cases, deviations from the guidelines should by all means be made.

Determining the Number of Option Shares Needed

A qualified stock option plan must be approved by the company's shareholders and must specify the number of shares reserved for option. Thus it is critically important to select a proper total-share figure—one which will be enough for the life of the plan, but which will not be excessive. Two methods may be employed.

The first involves an internal analysis of the company's probable needs. The granting guideline for each eligible's position is multiplied by the position's total compensation control point, and the resulting figures for all eligibles are totaled. This total amount is then multiplied by the number of years the plan will be in operation and by an estimated percentage to represent the average compensation escalation that will have occurred by the middle of the plan's life. The grand total thus derived is then divided by an estimate of the average option price per share over the entire plan life. The result is the number of shares that will be needed, assuming that overall executive performance is average.

The same procedure is run once again, but this time total compensation maximums are used rather than control points. The maximums determine the number of shares that will be needed, assuming that overall executive performance is outstanding. These two total-share figures give an indication of the range of probable internal needs.

The company should also examine the share-funding levels in other companies' plans. This can be done on a company-by-company basis, or broad industry survey information (such as is provided by the National Industrial Conference Board) can be analyzed. The figures produced by the internal and external comparisons should be similar. If they are not, the company may have to take appropriate action with respect to the size of its eligible group, for in those conflict situations that do occur, internal funding needs typically exceed those considered reasonable from an external standpoint, thereby pointing to an inflated eligible group.

Registering the Option Stock

Most companies register their option stock, but a number of companies are beginning to look envyingly at those that do not. Unregistered option stock requires an investment representation from the optionee before it can be exercised. This representation prevents the executive from selling his option stock except at a substantial discount for an indefinite period. (There is no hard rule as to when an investment representation is deemed to have lapsed, but most attorneys consider three years sufficient.) In the case of senior executives, an investment representation may be construed to extend to all the stock that the executive owns, including nonoption shares acquired earlier.

Thus we have an ingenious way of forcing executives

to hold on to their option stock—but it has its flaws. If he should quit, the executive may discover that his investment representation can be considered to have lapsed (because a substantial change in his employment conditions has taken place). In this case, the company has lost both the stock and the executive.

Because it is another negatively oriented motivational device, the use of unregistered stock is often bitterly resented by the company's optionees. And, since few companies use unregistered stock, the company's plan is automatically made less competitive.

Therefore, the use of unregistered shares is counterproductive. The costs of registration are not very high in absolute terms, and they are dirt cheap in relation to the costs of the stock option plan itself.

The Pressure to Hold

As implied, the use of unregistered shares is symptomatic of a larger problem: the desire of top management to have optionees hang on to their option stock.

There are two basic conflicts. The first is between the company and its shareholders and gets the company hung up on its own rhetoric. In most companies, the stock option plan is touted to the shareholders as a means whereby the executives, through stock ownership, will share the same personal objectives as the shareholders themselves. On the other hand, the company also knows that in practice the stock option is a well-deserved form of executive compensation. An executive who sells his option shares therefore goes against the expressed purpose of the stock option plan. And shareholders have been known to become quite displeased when a pattern of frequent "dumping" occurs. One valid reason for their anger is that issuance of new shares to fund an option plan (which is the usual practice) dilutes the holdings of the remaining shareholders. If these people are to have their equity diluted and lose the supposed motivational advantages of the plan to boot as a result of option stock sales, they have every reason to be angry.

The second conflict involves the individual optionee. He is given a huge grant of stock, which he may have considerable difficulty in financing, and is then expected to hold his shares no matter what. If he sells, he may receive a midnight phone call from the president, be passed over for promotion, or worse. As long as the stock rises meteorically, few problems will result. But if the stock drops meteorically, the executive is caught in a crunch between company loyalty and his own pocketbook.

He is already caught in such a crunch insofar as the Internal Revenue Service is concerned, because, if he sells his stock before he has held it three years or more, he loses the capital gains advantage on his spread. Nevertheless, as one executive put it, "I know that capital gains income is better than ordinary income, but, if it comes to a choice, ordinary income is better than no income!" The application of company pressure on top of IRS pressure is a terribly difficult burden for some executives to endure. Coupled with large grants of stock, this aspect of company pressure is somewhat analogous to holding out candy to a baby and then slapping his hand when he reaches for it.

Only about 20 percent of companies responding to a recent survey admitted that they place any pressure on the executive to retain his stock; but better than 40 percent of a group of individual executives reported feeling pressured. Curiously, the pressure seems to decrease markedly once the three-year qualifying period for capital gains tax treatment has passed. In effect, many companies have adopted the IRS rules as a convenient guideline for their own internal pressure policies.

Terminating the Option

IRS regulations state that a qualified stock option must expire no later than 90 days after termination of employment for reasons other than death and no later than one year after death. Most companies simply adopt the IRS language in designing their own plans.

Options should expire, however, on the date of termination if the individual is quitting voluntarily or is being discharged for cause. Allowing options for these people to continue for another 90 days simply gives them a free ride on any further appreciation. Considering the reasons for the terminations, such an approach makes no sense at all.

Allowing the 90-day post-termination period for cases of retirement, disability, and other such reasons is of course a sound procedure.

Individualizing Stock Options

A few progressive companies, such as General Motors and Du Pont, have developed what amounts to individualized option plans. A look at GM's plan will illustrate the approach used. Certain executives at GM receive a so-called contingent bonus in addition to their regular bonus. The former is one-third of the latter—or one-quarter of the total of both bonuses. Thus an executive who receives a $75,000 regular bonus may also receive a $25,000 contingent bonus, which is converted into shares of GM stock, essentially using the stock's current fair market value. Thus, if the stock were selling at $100 per share, the executive would receive a contingent bonus of 250 shares.

The GM executive's stock option is then based on the size of his contingent bonus: The executive receives three option shares for each contingent bonus share. In this instance, the option is for 750 shares. For each three option shares which the executive exercises during the five-year life of the option, one contingent bonus share is forfeited. Thus, if all 750 option shares are exercised, the executive will receive none of his 250 contingent bonus shares. On the other hand, if he exercises none of his option shares, he is paid his full 250 contingent bonus shares at the end of the five-year option period. It is left to the executive to choose the type of compensation he wants.

Under GM's three-shares-for-one-share formula, the point of indifference is theoretically reached when the option stock appreciates by 50 percent. Thus a 50 percent increase in the $75,000 worth of option stock used in our example would produce appreciation of $37,500. And this is exactly what the 250 contingent shares would be worth on the same day. From a practical standpoint, however, the decision as to whether to exercise the option stock or keep the contingent shares is not so simple, for the executive is unlikely to exercise his option stock and sell it the next day. He must consider such factors as the cost of financing his option; the three-year qualifying period (which if satisfied, can increase his after-tax yield above what is provided by the contingent shares); and the future outlook for the company's stock.

Nevertheless, the executive is given a degree of choice

between a smaller amount of relatively assured income and a larger amount of potential income. Here we have the risk versus reward principle put to good use.

Perhaps the reason so many companies shy away from GM's approach is that it involves an implicit cash valuation of an option's worth. Hence, an option at GM carries an initial value equal to one-third its aggregate option price. The fact that this may not be the correct value and that ascertaining the correct value is probably an impossible task may deter most companies from adopting this approach; obviously it hasn't deterred GM, which has had very good results.

Dividend Equivalents

The dividend equivalent is similar in some respects to the stock option. The executive is granted a number of units, each of which entitles him to a cash payment equal to the dividends declared on a share of common stock. The promise to pay varies in time from a few years at some companies to age 85 or death (whichever is the *later* event) at Du Pont.

Whereas the stock option is supposed to motivate the executive to work for an increase in the market value of the company's stock, the dividend equivalent is supposed to motivate him to work for an increase in the dividends—or at least to see that they don't decrease. Thus dividend equivalents, like stock options, seek to tie the executive's interests more closely to those of the shareholders.

The only problem with dividend equivalents is that they may end up motivating actions which are detrimental to the company's long-range interests. Thus the dividends may well be raised but the company may suffer from a lack of investment capital for new ventures.

Dividend equivalents have one thing going for them: their lack of visibility. If the executive is age 50, the dividend equivalents are payable until age 80; if the common stock dividend is currently $3 per share, each dividend equivalent may eventually give the executive $90 or more in compensation. (The dividends may go down, but that is rare nowadays.) Executives at companies that use dividend equivalents often possess thousands of them. Each alone is a trickle, but together they are a mighty river of compensation!

Restricted Stock

Until IRS took the fun out of it, a number of companies were exploiting the beauties of a compensation device known as restricted stock. Such stock could come in the form of a bonus or an option and entailed restrictions preventing its resale for a number of years (except back to the company at its original price). Its value was therefore flawed, and no tax was assessed on it until the restrictions lapsed. In that year, the executive was charged with ordinary income tax on the difference, if any, between the price he paid for it and the fair market value as of the date of the grant. When the stock was sold, he paid long-term capital gains taxes on any appreciation above the fair market value on the date of the grant. Moreover, if the stock declined to a point below its fair market value as of the date of grant but above its granting price, the difference between these points was used as the basis for tax payments.

Thus an individual could be given, say, an option in

restricted stock calling for an option price of $50 per share (when the fair market value of the stock was $100 per share), a term of exercise of ten years, and the lapse of restrictions shortly thereafter. If, at the time the restrictions lapsed, the stock had appreciated in value to $400 per share, the individual was taxed at ordinary income tax rates only on $50 (the amount of the discount from market as of the date of grant); and he received long-term capital gains tax treatment on the remaining $300 of appreciation.

Restricted stock, therefore, was clearly the best of both worlds. Used in an option, it gave the executive the capital gains tax treatment of a qualified stock option and the flexibility of option price and length of exercise period characteristic of a nonqualified option.

Compensation executives mounted the stump to proclaim the virtues of restricted stock. And as one enthralled observer remarked, "It's just too good to be true." Unfortunately, he was from the Internal Revenue Service! Shortly after it had given its blessing to restricted stock, IRS reversed its position and, with the aid of Congress, has dealt it a coup de grâce—at least from a tax standpoint.

Under the Tax Act of 1969, restricted stock is taxed at ordinary rates on its full market value as of the date the restrictions lapse if the stock is no longer subject to a substantial risk of forfeiture. However, lest someone accuse Congress of being ungenerous, there is also a provision which allows the executive to pay ordinary rates on the difference between market value as of date of grant and his purchase price, provided he does this within 30 days of the date of grant. Thereafter, he is entitled to long-term capital gains tax treatment on any subsequent appreciation. There is a hitch, though. Should the executive subsequently forfeit his stock, he cannot recover the taxes he has already paid.

Although the tax treatment on a restricted stock bonus is not different from the treatment on a deferred stock bonus, there may still be valid reasons for using restricted stock. The following story illustrates. Two Communists were conversing, and one said to the other, "If you owned two Chaiga automobiles, would you give one to your fellow Communist?" "Of course," replied the second. "A good Communist is always willing to share with his fellow Communist." "But what if you owned two refrigerators?" the first asked. "Naturally, I would do the same thing," was the answer. A series of further questions and identical answers ensued, involving television sets, stereos, and the like. Finally, the first Communist asked, "If you had two shirts, would you give one to your fellow Communist?" The second answered, "No I wouldn't." When asked why he said, "Because I have two shirts!"

This story illustrates that people fight harder to retain property they already have than that which they may or may not receive in the future. Giving the restricted stock certificates to an executive and allowing him to finger them gently each night before he goes to bed may have a very salutary effect.

8

The Cost-Effectiveness
of Stock Options

AS noted in Chapter 7, the option spread (the difference between the option price and the market value as of the date of exercise) in a qualified option represents the risk-free advantage that the executive has over the ordinary investor. Thus the option spread in a very real sense constitutes the executive's compensation from the option plan.

The special virtue of the qualified option plan is that if the executive holds the stock for at least three years, the option spread can be taxed at long-term capital gains rates. But, in order to obtain such capital gains tax treatment for its executive, *the company must lose its own corporate tax deduction on the compensation involved.*

In discussing this aspect of stock options, a number of executives have exclaimed, "What cost? What price? Qualified stock options don't cost me a cent. You show me the cost on my profit and loss statement." Now, it is true that, with the use of new shares, a company's after-tax profit remains unaffected by qualified stock option grants. On the other hand, the earnings per share decline because of the increase in the total number of shares outstanding.

At this point, the executive might again interject, "All right, so the earnings per share do go down, but the company has received extra cash from the sale of option stock. For my money, not only is there no cost, but the company gains through the extra cash." This is the same executive who, after selling his $2,000 car for $1,000, comes home bragging about his new-found supply of cash. "That's just wonderful, Henry," says his wife, "but where is the car?"

By the same token, a company must incur a cost any time it conveys property to someone else for less than it is worth. And the option spread, in the case of qualified stock options, is the amount of the cost. After all, had the company desired, it could have sold the stock on the open market and received the full proceeds from its sale, minus a modest underwriting fee.

Is it worth it for the company to forgo a tax deduction worth 48 cents on the dollar to give the executive an opportunity to cut his own tax rate through the use of capital gains taxation? The answer to this question determines whether stock options are a cost-effective compensation device for the company—in terms of holding down the after-tax cost of putting an after-tax dollar in the executive's pocket.

The cost-effectiveness of stock options can be calculated through the use of an oversimplified but substantially accurate formula:

$$\left(\frac{A}{B}\right) C = D$$

where A = the amount the executive nets from a dollar of
capital-gains-taxed compensation.

B = the amount the executive nets from a dollar
of ordinary income.

C = the company's after-tax cost of a dollar of
ordinary income paid to the executive.

D = the after-tax cost of placing the same amount
of money in the executive's pocket as he would
have received from a dollar of capital-gains-
taxed income.

To illustrate the use of this formula, let us take a hypothetical executive whose marginal tax bracket for additional
ordinary income is the maximum current tax rate of 70
percent. (All calculations are based on the laws in effect
prior to the Tax Reform Act of 1969. The impact of this
act is discussed shortly.) His tax rate for long-term capital
gains is therefore 25 percent, since capital gains taxes are
always one-half the ordinary rate or a maximum of 25 percent, whichever is lower. If our executive receives a stock
option, exercises it, and holds his stock for at least three
years, he stands to net 75 cents from each dollar of option
spread. This value is A in the equation.

On the other hand, if our executive receives a dollar of
additional ordinary income, he will net only 30 cents after
payment of taxes at a 70 percent rate. This value is B in
the equation.

If the executive were paid an additional dollar of ordinary income, the company could deduct it as a necessary
business expense (provided the payment was reasonable).
Since the corporate marginal tax rate is currently 48 percent, the company's net cost for this dollar of additional

223

income is 52 cents. This figure is C in the equation. Substituting these values,

$$\frac{\$0.75}{\$0.30} \times \$0.52 = D = \$1.30.$$

The company cannot deduct income on which the executive is taxed at capital gains rates. Thus the company's after-tax cost of $1 of capital-gains-taxed compensation is always $1. In our example, however, the use of ordinary income to offset the executive's capital gains advantage would cost the company $1.30—or 30 percent more—even after its tax deduction is figured. Thus the company could give the executive additional ordinary income of $2.50, which, after payment of taxes at the full 70 percent rate, would yield him the same 75 cents he would have received from $1 of capital-gains-taxed income. The company could then deduct the $2.50 payment from its corporate tax return, thereby lowering its net cost to $1.30 ($2.50 × 52 percent).

It appears, therefore, that stock options are certainly a cost-effective compensation device. But before casting this conclusion in concrete, let us take another example with different assumptions.

Our second executive has a marginal tax rate for additional ordinary income of 30 percent instead of 70 percent. His capital gains tax bracket is therefore 15 percent. The cost-effectiveness equation would be:

$$\frac{\$0.85}{\$0.70} \times \$0.52 = \$0.63.$$

In this example, it would cost the company only 63 cents after its tax deduction to offset the loss of capital gains tax treatment. In effect, the company could give the executive $1.22 of additional ordinary income, from which he would net 85 cents after payment of taxes at the full 30 percent rate. His yield is therefore no different from what he would have received from a dollar of capital-gains-taxed compensation. After deducting the $1.22 payment from its corporate tax return, the company's net cost would be lowered to 63 cents—a saving of 37 percent over the cost of a stock option.

Accordingly, we must modify our tentative conclusion to state that stock options represent a cost-effective device for some highly paid executives but not for other lesser-paid executives.

Cost-Effectiveness Breakeven Point

The cost-effectiveness breakeven point lies at a marginal tax bracket for additional ordinary income of 61 percent, as shown by the following:

$$\frac{\$0.75}{\$0.39} \times \$0.52 = \$1.$$

Thus the executive at a 61 percent tax bracket for additional ordinary income would net 75 cents from each dollar of capital-gains-taxed compensation at his prevailing 25 percent capital gains rate. To yield him the same 75 cents using ordinary income would require a payment of $1.93 ($1.93 × 39 percent yield from ordinary income = $0.75). After deducting this $1.93 from its corporate tax return, the company would incur a net cost of $1—or the same net cost it would have incurred from a qualified stock option.

A 61 percent tax rate for additional ordinary income doesn't exist, but a 60 percent tax rate applies when the individual's taxable income exceeds $88,000 per year. Assuming that the executive is married and has two dependent children and that his deductions are equal to 15 percent of his gross income, the pretax income (salary or bonus) needed before stock options become truly cost-effective is in the neighborhood of $106,000 per year.

This breakeven point would be overinflated if the executive were to sell a large amount of option stock in one year. His capital gains tax rate would remain at a steady 25 percent, but the costs to use an offsetting amount of ordinary income would soar because of the huge amount received in a single year. On the other hand, there are three other factors which suggest that the breakeven point may not be high enough.

First, although the executive's spread gives him an advantage over the ordinary investor, the fact that he has to hold the stock for three years to qualify for capital gains tax treatment represents a penalty vis-à-vis the ordinary investor, who must hold for only six months. Second, the fact that the executive must hold his stock for so long makes it all the more probable that he will have to borrow to finance his exercises. Although borrowing costs are reduced by dividends received and excess interest deducted, the executive still incurs some cost, and this eats into his capital gains advantage. With additional ordinary income, of course, the executive would probably have no borrowing costs whatsoever.

Third, the company often subjects its executives to intense pressure to retain their option stock. No such pressure exists for the ordinary investor. Pressure, in turn, may on occasion be translated into a decision to hold stock when, without the pressure, an opposite decision might have been made.

It is difficult to quantify some of these ancillary factors, but they obviously work in the direction of raising rather than lowering the cost-effectiveness breakeven point.

Trends in Cost-Effectiveness of Qualified Stock Options

Through the years, Congress has acted to make qualified stock options less and less cost-effective. Prior to the 1964 revenue act, ordinary income tax rates for both individuals and corporations were higher. Thus, with the predecessor restricted stock options, the cost-effectiveness breakeven point occurred at a 64 percent marginal tax bracket. Although this seemed nominally higher than the current 61 percent breakeven point, it was actually a lot lower because less income was required to reach it due to the steep rates that existed in those days. (The maximum rate was 91 percent versus the current 70 percent.)

The Tax Reform Act of 1969

The trend toward lessened cost-effectiveness reached its culmination in the Tax Reform Act of 1969, where it states that *qualified stock options will no longer be cost-effective at any income level. Moreover, in certain instances the effective tax rate on capital gains compensation will be higher than on an identical amount of ordinary income.*

Tax reform and tax complexity, it seems, are Siamese twins and cannot be separated. Prior to the Tax Reform

Act of 1969, the laws were, in retrospect, relatively simple. If the individual held his option stock for three years, the spread was taxable at long-term capital gains rates, which were a constant 25 percent once the executive's marginal ordinary bracket had exceeded 50 percent. Now as many as 13 possible tax consequences might result from the exercise and subsequent disposition of just one stock option grant.

Two of these consequences can occur in the year of exercise (under previous law, no tax effect occurred in that year). First, the amount of the spread that exceeds $30,000 plus the actual taxes the executive pays on his other income are taxed as a so-called preference item at a 10 percent rate. Second, the amount of the spread that exceeds $30,000 alone (not $30,000 plus actual taxes) reduces dollar for dollar the amount of earned income (salary, bonus, and so on) that can qualify for the maximum 50 percent tax.

Fortunately, both of these tax consequences are not likely to apply to the same executive at the same time. If his salary and bonus income are low, he is apt to get hit with the 10 percent preference tax, because the lower taxes on his other income produce a lower offset against the option spread. He will avoid the penalty on his earned income, because he is not yet up to a 50 percent bracket. On the other hand, if the executive's salary and bonus income are high, he may avoid the 10 percent preference tax but get hit by reduction of his earned income privilege.

Thus an executive whose tax bill on his salary and bonus income is $150,000 has to have an option spread of more than $180,000 ($150,000 plus $30,000) before the 10 percent preference tax comes into play. If his spread is only $130,000, he would therefore avoid this tax. However, he would not avoid a $100,000 penalty on his earned income privilege, because his spread exceeds the $30,000 offset alone by $100,000. If he has not exercised his option, that last $100,000 of taxable salary and bonus income would be taxed at only 50 percent.

If the 50 percent maximum privilege had not been enacted, however, this last slice would have been taxable at the normal 70 percent maximum rate, and that is just what happens in this instance. The result is that the executive's tax tab on his salary and bonus income is increased by approximately $20,000 (some further adjustments make the exact increase a slightly different figure).

Of course, if the option spread were exceedingly large (say $500,000 to $1,000,000), the executive could be affected by both of these tax consequences.

During the four years following exercise of his option, the executive can suffer residual penalties on his earned income privilege stemming from the original option exercise. The reason is that the penalty is stated as the greater of (1) the amount by which tax preference income for the current year exceeds $30,000 (and the option spread is just one of several types of tax preference income); or (2) the amount by which one-fifth of the aggregate tax preference income for the current and four preceding years exceeds $30,000.

Thus, an executive who exercises an option with a spread of $1,000,000 has $970,000 of penalty on earned income in the year of exercise, and $170,000 of penalty during the ensuing four years ($1,000,000 divided by 5 = $200,000 less the $30,000 offset = $170,000).

After suffering all these indignities, the executive comes to the year of disposition, which may be at least three years after the date of exercise. In this year, he is affected by one to three additional tax consequences. First, he is taxed

229

at long-term capital gains rates on the option spread and all subsequent appreciation occurring after the date of exercise. (The earlier taxes he pays prior to disposition do not affect his cost basis in the stock.) These capital gains rates have been raised by the Tax Reform Act of 1969. In 1972 and thereafter the rate will be a constant half of the applicable ordinary rate but no more than 25 percent on the first $50,000 of total gain. Thus, the maximum alternative tax of 25 percent has been severely limited. For example, if the executive is in a 70 percent ordinary tax bracket and has a $300,000 option gain, he will pay at the rate of 25 percent on the first $50,000 and 35 percent on the remaining $250,000. His total tax is therefore $100,000 —or 33.3 percent more than the taxes he would have paid prior to passage of the Tax Reform Act of 1969.

In addition, one-half of the net long-term capital gain (that is, the half that previously had been untaxed) becomes a tax preference item. Like the option spread, part of this amount can attract the 10 percent preference tax; or part of it can lower the earned income privilege; or both. Thus as many as two additional types of tax can be leveled on top of the capital gains tax.

Once again, the amount by which one-fifth of the tax preference items exceeds $30,000 lowers the earned income privilege in as many as four of the next four tax years. Ironically, the executive could find himself penalized twice in the same year by this provision, for in the year of disposition he could still be affected by the residual penalties from the year of exercise.

In sum, the net effect of these 13 possible tax consequences involving qualified stock options is to cause the effective tax rate on the option spread (that is, the total of all taxes attributable to the option divided by the gross option spread) to rise above 50 percent in some instances and to approach 50 percent in many other instances. Meanwhile, the maximum tax rate on salary and bonus income will be lowered to 50 percent in 1972. Considering the loss of corporate tax deductions on capital-gains-taxed option income, stock options are no longer going to be cost-effective to the company, no matter what the income level of the individual. And, to the extent that the effective tax rate exceeds 50 percent (or is so close to it as to wipe out borrowing costs), stock options aren't going to be very appealing to the individual executive either.

Impact on Earnings per Share

Suppose a company decided to apply the cost-effectiveness principles just discussed and replaced capital gains income with an offsetting amount of ordinary income for every executive whose marginal tax bracket indicated that such an approach was desirable. The result would be a slight drop in earnings per share during the first few years of such an approach, compared with the earnings per share that would have been obtained had only qualified stock options been utilized. By about the sixth year, however, the earnings per share would be back up to the level produced by the qualified stock option approach; and they would thereafter surpass those produced using only qualified stock options.

Actually, the company feels the effects of the cost of a qualified option share slowly, but it feels them forever, since the company has one more share outstanding. The cost of ordinary income, on the other hand, is written off completely in one year and thus represents a pay-as-you-go approach.

Replacing Qualified Options with Nonqualified Options

The cost-effectiveness lesson is simple: Companies that wish to maximize their earnings per share over the long term should eliminate executives' qualified stock options below the cost-effectiveness breakeven point and substitute a more cost-effective form of compensation. And, under the 1969 Tax Reform Act, this means eliminating qualified stock options entirely.

Thus progressive firms are turning more and more to nonqualified stock options, at least for their lower-paid executives (while retaining qualified options for the highest-paid executives). As noted in the preceding chapter, individuals are taxed at ordinary rates on nonqualified stock option spreads, and companies can deduct the amount of these spreads. Companies can gain the same apparent motivational advantages from nonqualified stock options as from qualified stock options, and at the same time they can adopt a highly cost-effective compensation posture.

Since nonqualified stock options have to be held for only six months after their exercise to qualify for long-term capital gains tax treatment, the executive is less likely to have to borrow substantial sums for a long period—provided, of course, that the company stops pressing him to hold his stock. This is a must if a nonqualified stock option plan is to be used. If the company implements a phantom stock option plan, it can also guarantee that the executive will not have to borrow anything.

Since the executive may not have to borrow, the company may not have to "gross up" his option size to offset the loss of his capital gains tax treatment. Two principles are involved here. First, the value of capital gains tax treatment increases as income levels rise. Thus, at a 30 percent tax bracket, the capital gains tax rate produces a 15-point advantage. At the 50 percent tax bracket, however, the capital gains tax rate produces a 25-point advantage.

Second, the net cost of interest charges declines with increasing income levels. Thus, with a 10 percent annual interest charge (which is not uncommon these days) and a 30 percent tax bracket, the net cost of interest is 7 percent, since 30 percent of the cost can be passed on to the federal government. At a 50 percent tax bracket, however, the net cost of a 10 percent annual interest payment is only 5 percent.

Both factors therefore work to favor the highly paid executive, who has a huge capital gains advantage and a low net interest cost; and both factors work against lower-paid executives, who have a small capital gains advantage and a high net interest cost. Moreover, it is the lower-paid executive who will most likely *have* to borrow to finance his option exercises.

To illustrate that net interest costs can wipe out capital gains tax savings at lower executive levels, assume that an executive whose marginal tax bracket for additional ordinary income is 30 percent receives $50,000 worth of option stock. Assume further that he exercises his option when the stock has appeciated to $75,000, that he borrows the entire $50,000 needed to finance his exercise, and that he pays an annual interest rate of 9 percent on the loan. The executive's spread is $25,000, and if he holds the stock for three years he stands to realize $21,250 after payment of capital gains taxes at a 15 percent rate. If instead he had received $25,000 in ordinary income, he would have realized $17,500 after payment of taxes at a 30 percent rate. Thus his capital gains advantage is $3,750.

Meanwhile, the executive must pay interest charges of 9 percent for three years. Part of these charges will, of course, be offset by the dividends he receives. Let us assume, therefore, that the company stock pays a dividend of 3.0 percent on market value but 4.5 percent for the executive (since he purchased the stock at one-third off). Therefore, the executive's interest costs in excess of dividends paid will be 4.5 percent. This excess can then be deducted by the executive and 30 percent of the cost passed on to the government. Thus, the net excess interest cost to the executive is 3.15 percent per year (4.5 × 70 percent) or $4,725 for three years ($50,000 principal × 3.15 percent × 3 years). These net interest costs exceed the capital gains tax savings of $3,750.

Of course, this example is somewhat overstated because the executive would probably be in a higher tax bracket at the time he actually sold the stock and would therefore have a greater capital gains tax savings. Moreover, if he took an equivalent amount of ordinary income all in one year, his marginal rate would rise substantially, although his capital gains rate would rise also.

Thus, by eliminating the necessity to borrow, the company can usually avoid grossing up ordinary income to offset the loss of capital gains tax treatment. The company's nominal compensation costs therefore remain the same, but, because it can now take advantage of its corporate tax deduction, its actual costs decline by a full 48 percent. The use of devices other than qualified stock options is therefore made even more cost-effective than indicated earlier, with the result that the recovery of and subsequent increase in earnings per share through the use of cost-effective compensation plans should be even speedier than previously described.

These increased earnings per share, of course, can be obtained only if treasury rather than open market shares are utilized. As noted earlier, the use of new shares in conjunction with deductible compensation devices places a double-barreled penalty on earnings per share—once in the form of lower net profits after taxes and once again in the form of a larger number of shares outstanding. Cash flow is increased, however, since the company has a deduction but no offsetting expenditure.

In using treasury shares, the company can fund its plan by purchasing the shares either when the options are exercised or when they are granted. In the first instance, the company merely buys the required number of shares on the open market and resells them to the individual when he wishes to exercise his option. The company's cost of purchase is partially offset by the proceeds from the option sale; the remainder (the spread) is then deducted.

On the other hand, the company could buy shares on the open market when grants are made to executives. At the time of exercise, the company gets back its initial expenditure and has a deduction on the spread with no accompanying expense (other than carrying costs between the dates of option grant and option exercise). In effect, the company is speculating on its own stock. If it is successful, the market pays for the costs of the option plan, while the company gains additional cash flow from its tax deduction. Of course, the stock may also go down!

Some companies do not use both qualified and nonqualified stock option plans to maximize cost-effectiveness because this approach is too complicated. In the view of top managers, it is simpler to employ qualified stock options for all executives; if some make a disqualifying disposition, so much the better, since the company will receive its tax deduction as a result of the executive's action.

But pressuring the executive to retain his stock on the one hand, while on the other hand hoping he will sell it within three years' time, creates a conflict. More important, the company has lost control of its tax deduction. It is now the executive who decides whether the company is going to obtain a deduction. And, more often than not, he will be prompted to go for capital gains taxation, not because it may actually be rewarding (considering the financing costs), but because it *appears* rewarding.

Motivational Problems of Stock Options

Stock options present certain motivational problems in addition to those concerning their cost-effectiveness. The compensation an executive receives from a stock option (his spread) is determined by three factors: the size of his grant, the market behavior of the stock, and his sagacity as an investor. Let us examine each of these.

First, the size of the stock option grant is totally under the company's control, and, if granting guidelines such as the ones discussed earlier are employed, the size of the grant can be made both competitive and equitable.

Second, the market price of the stock is dependent on a number of variables, only one of which—earnings per share—is under the control of the company's management. Governmental policies, inflation, recession, war, and a host of other variables which affect stock prices are outside the company's control.

Total responsibility for earnings per share, in turn, is typically assigned to only two executives: the chairman and the president, who control only pretax earnings per share. Everyone else has an even smaller piece of the action. Considering the many contaminants affecting market behavior, the correlation between the chairman's and president's performance and the market price of the company's stock is sometimes marginal.

For other executives, the correlation between their performance and the market price of the company's stock is undoubtedly spurious—and sometimes negative. Thus we have the division manager whose operations went "down the tubes" when the rest of the company was racking up a substantial increase in earnings per share. Likewise, we have the division manager who did a superlative job in a year when the rest of the company was moribund.

If an executive's performance and the compensation he receives from his stock options are not closely related, then there is little motivational value to stock options. If the probability of receiving a reward is equal whether one changes one's behavior or not, then there is little incentive to change. For compensation to motivate, therefore, the executive must feel that the control he exercises over his own performance directly influences the rewards he receives.

There is some concrete evidence to support these theoretical contentions, such as the case of Ling-Temco-Vought, Inc. Although James Ling's primary purpose in creating a degree of public ownership in each of his subsidiaries was not to motivate his executives, he did derive some motivational value from the move. The relationship between an executive's performance and his awards is more direct in a publicly held subsidiary than it is in a corporate giant such as LTV: What he does may have a considerable impact on the stock's per-share earnings and therefore on the market prices of the subsidiary's stock. The better his performance, the greater the likelihood that his option shares will increase in value. On the other hand, the performances of all the other subsidiaries would also be reflected in the per-share earnings and therefore in the market price of the parent company's stock. The executive's impact on corporate profitability is trifling compared with his impact on his own subsidiary's profitability, so the motivational value of stock in the parent corporation is far less than the motivational value of stock in the publicly held subsidiary. Mr. Ling has since recognized that he gained a great advantage and has touted it to others.

Now we find that some companies are making motivation the primary reason for creating a market for their subsidiaries' stock. For example, in describing the management philosophy of David Mahoney, president and chief executive of Norton Simon, Inc., *Business Week* reported: "Eventually, large divisions could sell some stock to the public—less to raise revenues than to provide division management with incentive stock options in the part of the company over which they have the most control."

There are two key words in this statement: "incentive" and "control." As already noted, without control, there can be little incentive. And by implication, the use of an approach other than the one recommended by Mr. Mahoney offers little possibility of executive control.

Additional evidence as to the motivational problems of stock options comes from companies whose option stock has gone "under water"—that is, the market value of the stock has plummeted below the option price. Many of these companies were once stock market favorites and commanded extremely high and growing price–earnings multiples. As long as the stock was moving up, the executives of these companies were quite happy with their option plans, as indeed they should have been. But with the downward trend came executive grumbling; when the options "submerged," the grumbling turned into a high-decibel wail.

Interviews with some of these executives produced such comments as this: "These options are no measure of my performance. The guys in division X loused us all up. The company ought to come up with something that rewards me for *my* contributions." As in an ancient Chinese proverb, "Victory has a thousand fathers and defeat has none."

This attitude on the part of executives is further demonstrated by the Booz, Allen & Hamilton survey cited earlier. Of the executives questioned, 57 percent said they thought the relationship between their performance and their option rewards was moderate or weak. About the same percentage also thought that their option rewards were not high enough. Translation: Options are motivational only when they produce a lot of money for the optionee.

The third factor affecting the rewards the executive will receive from his stock options involves his sagacity as an investor. To illustrate, assume that two executives were each granted $50,000 worth of option stock. The first executive exercised his option two years after it was granted, when the market price of the stock was $75,000. This executive's spread, and hence his compensation, was therefore $25,000. The second executive delayed his exercise until two months prior to the expiration of the option's five-year term, at which time the stock had appreciated to $100,000. The second executive's compensation was therefore $50,000.

Both executives started with the same option, yet one made twice as much as the other. Unfortunately, the executive who gained more was not necessarily the better performer; he was merely a more astute investor. Sagacity as an investor, while undoubtedly admirable, should not be the reward criterion in a company's executive compensation package.

Creating separate markets for subsidiary stock is a partial solution to the motivational problem of stock options, but we still have the contaminants that are not subject to the division manager's control. And we still have executives reporting to the division manager who, unlike him, have only a piece of the earnings-per-share action. What, then, is the answer?

For motivational reasons, stock options should be entirely abandoned for all but the top two or three executives (and the top executive in each subsidiary if a separate market is created). For motivational and cost-effectiveness reasons, qualified options even for these top executives should be abandoned.

This does not mean that there should be no other form of compensation to take the place of options. The company must always remain competitive, and there are always going to be some companies with option plans.

Alternative Approaches

Devices to replace stock options are limitless once the company decides to subordinate taxation to motivation—

not the reverse. For example, the company can, as described earlier, include long-range objectives in its bonus plan and then increase its award ranges to offset the abandonment of the stock option plan.

Or the company can grant large blocks of restricted stock to key executives and tie the retention of these shares to distant and quantifiable performance targets. For example, one company recently gave a vice-president better than $1 million of restricted stock, with the restrictions set to lapse in 25 years. Whether the man gets to keep that stock, however, will depend on the cumulative performance of the divisions under his command over the next ten years.

Thus sales must be increased at a compounded annual rate of 30 percent a year—and so must profits. The average annual return on invested capital must be 35 percent before taxes. Obviously, these are highly demanding targets. But then, $1 million is a lot of money. If the goals are achieved, both the vice-president and the company will win—and that, after all, is the basis of a symbiotic relationship. If the goals are not achieved, the executive will have to return all or some portion of the stock to the company. Since the certificates are already in his safe deposit vault, the act of giving them up would be excruciatingly painful. This is another reason why he will do everything possible to see that he keeps them.

With such an approach, the company can control the executive's initial reward. The extra reward he may eventually receive through appreciation of his stock, while possibly exceeding the initial reward, is a secondary consideration, since he could have realized the same appreciation as an ordinary investor by buying and retaining an equivalent number of shares.

Consider another alternative to stock options. Dividend

equivalents were discussed earlier but were dismissed because they might actually work to trigger an increase in dividends when such action would be ill-advised. That would diminish their appeal. Raising dividends may not always be in the stockholders' long-term interests, but raising earnings per share always is. Therefore, why not consider a new form of compensation involving the payment of earnings-per-share equivalents? To introduce a longer-range form of motivation, these equivalents could be predicated not on a single year's earnings per share but on the cumulative earnings per share of several years. They could also be based on pretax earnings per share if desired and could employ a threshold limitation to prevent their payment when earnings per share were less than excellent.

For example, a plan of this nature might be based on the cumulative earnings per share that are actually attained during the ensuing five years (that is, five separate earnings-per-share figures added together). It might be further specified that unless this cumulative figure were, say, $15 or more, no awards would be made. Thereafter, each unit granted to an executive would entitle him to the actual cumulative earnings per share attained by the company and would be payable to him either in a lump sum or after retirement, according to his preference.

For divisionalized companies, the earnings-per-share equivalents could be predicated on divisional contributions to earnings per share or a weighted combination of divisional contributions and overall corporate results.

Such a plan would provide a very healthy check on excesses that might arise from the company's bonus plan. In the latter plan, the executive is rewarded for attaining immediate results. In the former, he is rewarded for attaining longer-range results. Without this plan, he might be tempted to maximize current profits at the expense of the company's future. With both plans, he is given an incentive to achieve an equitable blend of current profits and longer-term results.

Of utmost importance, by varying his performance, the executive can control the amount of the reward he will receive. And thus we have compensation at its motivational best.

All this does not suggest that qualified stock options (or any other options) are dead. In some cases they will remain alive despite the Tax Reform Act of 1969—for example, when the company's organization is centralized and its stock's market value is in high correlation with earnings per share; when the company needs capital and is unable to borrow or make public offerings of its stock; when the company cannot sustain a lowering of its after-tax profits through deduction of nonqualified spreads and phantom stock payments.

The one point it is most important to understand is that the tax problems of qualified stock options and the motivational problems of all stock options make it impossible to justify option plans simply because 80 percent of *other* companies use them. An automobile manufacturer's selling campaign was once built around the slogan: "One million owners can't be wrong." That automobile was the Packard.

9

Epilogue

MANY topics have been discussed in this book, including the assessment of executive performance, the design of integrated total compensation structures, the use and abuse of executive bonus plans, the possibilities and pitfalls of deferred compensation, and the problems inherent in stock option plans.

Throughout, one word has occurred with great frequency: *motivation*. This has been the subject of the book and should be the purpose of executive compensation.

Taxes are important to executive compensation. Technique is important. But motivation is *paramount*. To achieve it requires that

★ Reward opportunities be meaningful and commensurate with the risks involved.

* Rewards vary with demonstrated performance so that the executive knows he can control his rewards by controlling his performance.

The concepts are simple; the execution is not. But the job is well worth trying, for the successful motivation of increased executive performance is always superbly rewarding.

Index

About the Author

GRAEF S. CRYSTAL is associated with Towers, Perrin, Forster & Crosby, Inc., where he is in charge of the company's executive compensation consulting services in the New York area. He manages executive compensation studies covering such areas as base salary design and administration, executive incentive compensation, stock options, and executive perquisites. He received his A.B. in industrial psychology from the University of California at Berkeley and his M.A. in the same field from Occidental College.

Mr. Crystal has served as senior associate with Booz, Allen & Hamilton Inc. He has also held positions at General Dynamics and Pfizer International, Inc. where he was responsible for corporate compensation policies and programs. In addition, Mr. Crystal has conducted studies in sales incentive compensation in a wide variety of industries.

Mr. Crystal has contributed chapters to *Compensating Executive Worth, Personal Financial Planning for Executives, Corporate Growth Strategies,* and *Management Handbook,* all published by AMA. He is a member and former vice-president of the American Compensation Association.